LIFELINES

EDITH SCHAEFFER

Lifelines

The Ten Commandments For Today

CROSSWAY BOOKS ● WESTCHESTER, ILLINOIS
A DIVISION OF GOOD NEWS PUBLISHERS

Lifelines: The Ten Commandments for Today, copyright © 1982 by Edith Schaeffer. Published by Crossway Books, a division of Good News Publishers, 9825 West Roosevelt Road, Westchester, Illinois 60153.

Cover design: The Cioni Artworks/Ray Cioni.

First printing, 1982.

Printed in the United States of America.

Library of Congress Catalog Card Number: 81-71468

ISBN: 0-89107-228-4

CONTENTS

INTRODUCTION:
Why the Ten Commandments?

Eighteen-month-old Debby bent over lower and lower beside her kitten, tucking her knees under her, but back a bit so that gradually she could parallel kitty's curve to the dish. Slowly, as Debby watched kitty's movements, she carefully duplicated them as exactly as she could until suddenly her tongue was making an exact copy of kitty's fast, rough tongue lapping up the prescribed cat food with deft little jerks. It wasn't many seconds before Debby's mother put aside her astonished interest in what was going on and gathered her growing child lovingly into her arms to sit down and explain something. "Darling, funny little person, you are not a kitty cat, you are a little girl. That is cat food, made especially to be good for cats, but is *not* what Mummy wants you to eat. Look, you have a lovely poached egg on toast, orange juice, some nice toast fingers, and raspberry yogurt. Let me put you in your chair and you can eat it now—with your fingers or with these nice spoons and forks. You can have a flower on your table because you like to look at something pretty as well as to eat something that tastes good. Do you want Mummy to put on this music, or to read you a story? See this book? Would you like to listen to this story while you eat? Good. MMMMmmmm—that was a big hug and kiss. You are such a nice little girl, and there are lots and lots of things to learn about *who* you are, and *what* the differences are between being a little girl and a kitty."

"Who am I?"

"How can I be fulfilled?"

These questions come in wailing whines, wistful voices, screaming anger, honest confusion, in frustrated search, in determined research, or in willful rebellion. How are people supposed to find the answers? How are people supposed to know who they are, and how they can be fulfilled?

Patterns for people and their behavior are being purposely twisted by some who want to stamp out the truth of what is, who want to hit their heads against the stone wall of what really exists as they shout that the wall and the stone—and even their heads—are not there! Sitting on a bench outside the Roman Baths in Bath, England, a group of Punks (with no two alike) displayed heads shaved in various patterns, faces painted shades of green or purple, eyebrows shaved off or safety pins in their cheeks and rings in their noses. They were, after all, not so original, because through the centuries there have been rebels against behaving, looking, speaking the truth of what the world really is, and who human beings really are. Through the centuries people have turned away deliberately from the true and living Creator who has told them who they are and have turned to gods who did not make them, but who are as Jeremiah tells us, "like scarecrows in a melon patch." If people are going to make false gods and then fool themselves and others into believing that they exist and then worship them, meditate about them, talk to them, and sing about them . . . then they are going to be *like* these gods in their behavior and even in their twisted lack of understanding as to who they are. Just as acting like a kitty cat does not make a child into a cat, acting like something other than a person really is does not make that person able to be fulfilled by another set of things. What is, is. This is not only a profound statement; it explains why the psychiatrists' offices are full in country after country, as well as explaining many other kinds of misery and frustration. People are trying to be what they are *not* made to be, and relate to what does *not* exist.

God has said that He made people. He knows who they are. He made them male and female—two kinds, with gorgeous diversity and endless variety to be enhanced, tenderly cared for, creatively developed, not erased. He made them in His image, to think and act and feel, to be able to have ideas and choose among them in order to create, to love and to be compassionate, to understand other people as well as themselves, to communicate abstract ideas as well as concrete ideas, to write as well as verbalize audibly, to relate to other people on a horizontal level as well as to relate to Him, the Infinite One. He made them with the capacity to be parents, knowing tender compassion and love toward children, experiencing the relationship of generations, having a capacity for continuity. God made people in His image with endless capacity; yet they were finite and limited in comparison to His infiniteness. God had no beginning. He was there, is there, will be there. He is the Creator. He had to be there to create. The very statement that He is the Creator says He was there. He made people to live forever, but He did not make them as programmed computers, or puppets to be manipulated. He gave them choice, and choices have results.

There is cause and effect history. That history is real, and we are affected by the past, as well as the present and our knowledge of something of the future. We live in the midst of history; our feet dangle in the stream of history. It does not pass us as a river that we never put a foot in: we swim in it, we boat in it, our feet dangle in it, we get wet in it. History surrounds us, and we affect history. History is *our* history, at least the period we have been born and live in, as well as the period that affects us before our birth, and the period we are affecting after our death. People need to know all this to know even the tiniest beginning of an answer to Who am I? and How can I be fulfilled?

There was a list of one commandment in the beginning. It was made to Adam before Eve was made. First it was one commandment for one person; then it was one commandment for two persons. It could have been the only commandment, or rule for behavior, or regulation for living, if only it had been kept, observed, obeyed, believed, respected. But it wasn't. God had said that He was giving all kinds of freedoms: to be fruitful and increase in number, to rule over the fish and birds and animals, to eat a stupendous variety of fruit, vegetables, melons, and so on. But He had given one strong negative commandment: "You are free to eat from any tree in the garden; but you must not eat from the tree of the knowledge of good and evil, for when you eat of it you will surely die." If Adam and Eve had not eaten, there would have been no death, no deterioration. If they had obeyed and respected and believed the Word of God in that commandment, there would have been no abnormality. But they did, and the world, people, animals, all nature has been spoiled, devastated. God's perfect creation has been vandalized and spoiled. Death has come in like a flood spilling out of a broken dam. Ugliness has blotted out much that was beautiful. None of us has ever seen perfection in nature, in human beings, or in relationships and situations. Since the breaking of that first law, people have needed some kind of explanation about how to get along with each other, as well as fulfilling what God made them to be.

So God gave other directions, through His prophets and His servants, at different times of history. When God gives directions, they don't clash. They are true to what is, because He is the Creator. When the rules and regulations are made by changing religions, changing cultures, changing periods of history, they are all some form of directions coming from man-made gods. Thus they clash with what is, and they clash with the questions, Who am I? and What will fulfill me? and What can I do that will fit into the framework of what really is true? Men and women have made up their own rules, or they follow someone else's made-up rules, and it simply does not work. It is like banging your head against a wall that really is there while singing a song that goes, "It isn't there, ouch . . . it isn't there, ouch . . . it isn't there at all, at all, *ouch, OUCH!*"

Jeremiah explains it like this (Jeremiah 10:1-5, 12-16):

Hear what the Lord says to you, O house of Israel. This is what the Lord says: "Do not learn the ways of the nations or be terrified by the signs in the sky, though the nations are terrified by them. For the customs of the people are worthless; they cut a tree out of the forest, and a craftsman shapes it with his chisel. They adorn it with silver and gold; they fasten it with hammer and nails so it will not totter. Like a scarecrow in a melon patch, their idols cannot speak; they must be carried because they cannot walk." . . . But God made the earth by his power; he founded the world by his wisdom and stretched out the heavens by his understanding. When he thunders, the waters in the heavens roar; he makes clouds rise from the ends of the earth. He sends lightning with the rain and brings out the wind from his storehouses. Everyone is senseless and without knowledge; every goldsmith is shamed by his idols. His images are a fraud; they have no breath in them. They are worthless, the objects of mockery; when their judgment comes, they will perish. He who is the Portion of Jacob is not like these, for he is the Maker of all things, including Israel, the tribe of his inheritance—the Lord almighty is his name.

What a clear picture God gave to Jeremiah and to the people in his time! And God has preserved it for us so that we can understand something of our time. The Punks are following a scarecrow in a melon patch, so of course they come to look like that. This is true of all who rebel against the Creator of the universe, the Judeo-Christian God of the Bible who made all things, and made people so that they could be in relationship with Him as well as with each other. The rebellion against Him ends in rebellion against what He has designed people to enjoy and to be fulfilling to them.

Jeremiah prays later in that same chapter: "I know, O Lord, that a man's life is not his own; it is not for man to direct his steps."

Many different kinds of direction are needed because there are many different ways to be lost. Physical direction is needed by people who have lost their way in a city, in the woods, on a lake or river, on the high seas, in the mountains, crossing deserts, in rocky places, or in endless fields of corn. Philosophical direction is needed to understand something about the meaning of life. Moral direction is needed to understand how to act toward other people and toward God.

When God gave that first commandment, our first parents were surrounded by all the positive things of that perfect garden with its endless provision of everything that was needed for life and creativity—love, family, fulfillment, and a daily possibility of communicating with Him. When it came to the time of Moses and God gave what is known as the Ten Commandments, they were given in the midst of the marvelous experiences of going through the Red Sea, of seeing the water gush forth from the rock in a time of thirstiness, of being fed balanced food that fell each day for their need of nourishment, as well as in the midst of promises for the future. God gave explanations along with the Ten Commandments and placed them in the framework of His Word, the Bible. This framework kept filling out as a house that is first a frame, then filled in with wood, stone, glass, plaster, brass, tiles, and so on until it is complete. The frame is always needed; the understanding increases gradually as to what part each portion of the "house" has in the completed whole.

If the people of the world, after the fall, had not turned to false gods, they at least would have known what was right and wrong. Had there been no rebellion and turning from the true and living God to a variety of "scarecrows," everyone would have known about Him, His existence, His commands, His explanations, His directions, His promises, and His preparations for our future. Everyone would have known what things are really wrong. Everyone would have had the right kind of "mirror" to see the dirt on his or her face and would have been aware of the need of a "bath," a "wash," to be clean. Everyone would have had God's explanations as to what is right and what is wrong.

Now don't misunderstand. Because of the cause and effect history following the rebellion of Adam and Eve, *no one could perfectly follow God's commandments*. But there is a big difference between *seeing that you have done wrong* and *not knowing that there is a wrong*, and thinking there is no standard for right and wrong at all, or following the rules of one of the false gods, one of the scarecrows, one of the idols made with men's hands or with people's imaginations. God spoke very strongly about how to make it possible for people to know the law, to know not only the Ten Commandments but His full Word, including all He has done to help people know He is indeed God, and that He is all-powerful and infinite and compassionate, and that His law is worth knowing, remembering, thinking about, and talking about.

Come to Deuteronomy. Moses has given the law to the people, the Ten Commandments God wrote on the tables of stone. Now Moses is telling the people how extremely important it is to explain these laws to the children, and also to answer their children's questions, and to discuss and talk with them about all that God did in the time before they were born, as well as earlier in their own lives. These parents were to keep their communication with God and with their children current, so that it did not become a stale repetition. Listen:

"These are the commands, decrees and laws the Lord your God directed me to teach you to observe in the land that you are crossing the Jordan to possess, so that you, your children and their children after them may fear the Lord your God as long as you live by keeping all his decrees and commands that I give you, and so that you may enjoy long life. Hear, O Israel, and be careful to obey so that it may go well with you and that you may increase greatly in a land flowing with milk and honey, just as the Lord, the God of your fathers, promised you. Hear, O Israel: the Lord our God, the Lord is one. Love the Lord your God with all your heart and with all your soul and with all your strength. These commandments that I give you today are to be upon your hearts. Impress them on your children. Talk about them when you sit at home and when you walk along the road, when you lie down and when you get up." (Deut. 6:1-7)

This is crystal clear: Children are not to be told "run along and don't ask questions." Children are to be included in family discussion concerning the law of God and past history related in God's revelation. They are also to be included as the family studies God's Word as it relates to current things that are discussed during breakfast, as the morning paper is being read, or on a walk as the day's events are thought of in the city streets, or in fields, burning up with too much sun or covered with volcano dust or rotting with too much rain. God's law, God's Word, the Ten Commandments are to be related to the present moment of history, because these are the Living Words of God and applicable right to the very end of the age when the big change comes. And they should be a natural part of conversation. However, families also need to discuss realities of answered prayer that are not as startling as the Red Sea rolling back, but are part of their family history of living as sheep of His pasture.

Today, many people say there is no absolute, there is no God who has ever spoken. Others feel that even if He does exist, whatever His Word was centuries ago, it must be changed now. It is outdated in our day of computers, electronic devices, packaged meals, instant gratification, throwaway plastic or paper products.

Words like "continuity" and "lasting" and "unchanging" seem to be blurred with dust, only to be thought of as some antique concept to be a bit nostalgic about, but not to be taken seriously.

When things from the past are discarded and God's law is spurned, the Ten Commandments are thought to be obsolete. Unhappily, even believers who reverence God's Word sometimes feel that the Ten Commandments can be pushed aside and forgotten, with no recognition of the balance of the whole of God's Word, the entire teaching of the whole Bible.

What Have We Missed in Not Studying the Ten Commandments?
As an introduction to the Ten Commandments, Psalm 19 presents a vivid picture of what God would have us understand and "feed upon" as well as live by and be refreshed with.

> The law of the Lord is perfect,
> > reviving the soul.
> The statutes of the Lord are trustworthy,
> > making wise the simple.
> The precepts of the Lord are right,
> > giving joy to the heart.
> The commands of the Lord are radiant,
> > giving light to the eyes.
> The fear of the Lord is pure,
> > enduring forever.
> The ordinances of the Lord are sure
> > and altogether righteous.
> They are more precious than gold,
> > than much pure gold;
> they are sweeter than honey,
> > than honey from the comb.
> By them is your servant warned;
> > In keeping them there is great reward.
> Who can discern his errors?
> > Forgive my hidden faults.
> Keep your servant also from willful sins;
> > may they not rule over me.
> Then will I be blameless,
> > innocent of the great transgression.
> May the words of my mouth and the meditation of my heart
> > be pleasing in your sight,
> > O Lord, my Rock and my Redeemer. (vv. 7-14)

What a marvelous prayer of David's to sing and to pray along with him! In order to have any idea of our errors, our faults, our sins, hidden as well as willful, we need to *know* and *think* about the law of God, His Word to us. The prayer to God as Redeemer is fantastic in its understanding. How was it possible to have sins forgiven and to be redeemed? There needed to be knowledge of sin in order to know what to ask forgiveness for, because no one was able, or ever is able, to keep the law perfectly. However, there has always been a way of redemption set forth. Even in Old Testament times, David understood that His redeemer was a person, the Messiah to come. He understood that when the law was broken, he needed to bring a lamb, which would be like the ram caught in the thickets, the substitute for Isaac which enabled Abraham to go back down the mountain with his son's hand in his. The only One who was alone altogether, and who had to die Himself as the substitute, was the Messiah who fulfilled all these promises. He was the Redeemer and Rock David looked for and praised, and He also is our Rock and Redeemer when we come to know Him.

Then if we are redeemed and the laws and commandments we have each broken are something we are forgiven for, why do we need to read the Word of God continually, including the commandments wherever in the Bible they occur?

We don't get whisked off to heaven the moment we have found forgiveness, and in Paul's words in Romans we see a value, a reason, a purpose, a meaning, an importance (something which brings real results) in our day by day living *before* we reach heaven. The important things we have to *do* must be accompanied by the important things we are meant to *be*. A balanced diet of reading, talking about, discussing, meditating upon, studying, enjoying, discovering fresh things, fresh concepts, fresh helps for the day, is basic in both doing and being, both the "action based on faith" and the "growing in faith" which is meant to be what the Christian life is all about.

A balanced understanding of the whole Bible, which is never complete but which should increase throughout the short years of our lives, needs to include an understanding of what the Ten Commandments mean in my life and in yours, no matter what our age, where we live, and what we do for a living, or how much we are subjected to as we live in the smog of this present penetrating monolithic spread of ideas, coming forth from the present forms of "scarecrows in the cornfields."

The questions Who am I? and How can I be fulfilled? can only be answered by the Creator. Since we have no perfect person to look to as a pattern because all have been imperfect since Adam's fall, the Ten Commandments and the speaking of God in history through His revealed Word have been given so that we *could* find out what we need to know.

When the Messiah, Jesus, the Son of God, came in person to walk among people and to demonstrate perfection to them, He kept the Law perfectly, and helped all who have lived since to understand it more completely; but He did not erase the law. In Matthew, Jesus in the Sermon on the Mount speaks strongly:

> "Do not think that I have come to abolish the Law or the Prophets; I have not come to abolish them but to fulfill them. I tell you the truth, until heaven and earth disappear, not the smallest letter, not the least stroke of a pen, will by any means disappear from the Law until everything is accomplished. Anyone who breaks one of the least of these commandments and teaches others to do the same will be called least in the kingdom of heaven, but whoever practices and teaches these commands will be called great in the kingdom of heaven. For I tell you that unless your righteousness surpasses that of the Pharisees and the teachers of the law, you will certainly not enter the kingdom of heaven."

Now you may say, "Oh, but I thought the blood of the Lamb took away all sin, and that all our righteousness is as filthy rags so that the only righteousness that counts is Christ's righteousness, which covers us as white linen." And you are right, that is given to us. But we are not to ignore the importance placed on our recognizing right from wrong today and asking for help to live more and more in accordance with God's standards in all parts of life. Will we ever be perfect in this life? No. But the standard is still in place. It is meant to be part of our conversation and our meditation, our teaching and our discussion, our practice and our base for living.

Come to the 119th Psalm. Come to the riches it spills out as a white waterfall of prayer splashing into the whole sea of our daily life. Stand under the flow and feel the force and sparkling refreshment of its words and make some of this your prayer, day after day, time after time, in one situation and another—not as trite religious words, but as part of the marvel of "joining in" with those who have prayed in other centuries with some of the same insights that will be yours. Read at least a portion of it now.

As we read the 119th Psalm think of how often you and I turned toward selfish gains, not only in material things but in spiritual things, not only in emotional things but in physical things. How often we have turned toward using our Christianity as a thing of gain for selfish motives, rather than a desire to please God and worship Him and do some measure of His will. By choosing the way of truth, how much time have we spent in finding out how *much* He has forgiven us for, and how we can strive to turn away from worthless things and live more in accordance with His Word?

Perfection? God does say, "Be ye perfect, even as your Father in heaven is perfect," and Jesus continues in Matthew 5 to explain more of what He means when He says that He has not come to abolish the law. Yet, it is made clear that although perfection is the goal, in being closer to what we were made to be in the first place, perfection is not going to be completed, is not going to be a reality hour by hour, day by day, week by week, until Jesus comes back and we are changed, and all nature is restored.

But just because we can't achieve perfection is no excuse for any of us to stop studying the law of God, the Ten Commandments, the Way the Lord has outlined as the way of life for His children to follow. However, in teaching or discussing the law of God, we can never sit above people thundering down at them, our own children or our grandchildren, our neighbors or friends, our congregation or the employees under us, our enlisted men if we are officers, our students if we are professors. In considering and probing into the meaning of the whole Word of God, and the Ten Commandments in the context of that whole Word, in relationship to our moment of history and particularly each of us in our own set of circumstances in our own spot of geography, we each one sit together on the same level of seats! We sit *under* the law along with everyone else. We sit under the teaching of the Word of God, considering our own failings even as we suddenly become aware of others' failings. We take our place on very low benches under the Judge who is the only Judge, the very One who tells us, "Judge not that ye be not judged." At the same time, He is urging us to talk about His law, His commands, His direction as to how to live, to generation after generation.

It will be no excuse that we misinterpreted "judge not that ye be not judged" as meaning we were to never make truth known, and never portray a contrast so that people *could* see the difference between the law of the true God who is the Creator and the false gods whose laws are as much a caricature of God as "the scarecrow in the cornfield" is in setting forth standards, or making pronouncements or promises! Now go back to Psalm 119. Be spurred on to actively loving God's laws, which are to help us be whom He made us to be, as well as to do what He made us to do.

People today are all mixed up in twisted ideas. They live in a welter of garbled voices, looking for directions from papers that come floating down like Alice in Wonderland's cards, scattered like blown leaves all about her. Although these papers are in different languages, from different thought-forms, different philosophies, all say that there is no truth and no absolute upon which to live, no base for any choice of a moral standard. So whether one reads the papers upside down, left to right, knows one word in three, it doesn't matter. There'll be a new wind in a few days to blow more into one's head. Perhaps you can even stop looking for papers among the falling leaves. Just turn to the last piece of television advice, given in the most colorful or unforgettable way—whatever has stuck in the memory. One way is as good as any other! All law is obsolete. There are no more standards.

Living in the midst of such neighbors we need to be spurred on to actively loving God's laws which He carefully handed down to us, and which were meant to be handed on from generation to generation. Living in the midst of such a monolithic anti-God humanism that affects all thinking and speaking, singing and painting, writing and doing business, we need to be sure that the whole family spends time together making fresh discoveries of what God's law is all about.

Yes, do come back to Psalm 119, verse 43: "Do not snatch the word of truth from my mouth, for I have put my hope in your laws."

Continuity is the unmistakable ingredient of God's Word, God's truth, God's pronouncements, God's revelation. Such words as eternal, everlasting, boundless, enduring, such concepts as all generations, enduring earth, enduring laws, changeless faithfulness, unending love have no place in a relativistic, constantly changing world. The flood of broken relationships are born naturally out of the flood of broken concepts. People are handed shreds of ideas like broken glass to fit together which will never fit together and which cut their hands in the attempt.

God, who created all things, to whom we can say, "Your hands made me and formed me; give me understanding to learn your commands" (119:73), is a Person and made me and you in His image as persons too, able to communicate, able to relate with a measure of understanding. Can the finite relate to the infinite? Can the limited relate to the unlimited? Can the now spoiled relate to the perfectly unspoiled? Of course, there are limitations. But God has made it possible for us to relate to Him, to understand Him, to know Him, to communicate with Him, in a growing measure, in truth and reality, because He is a Person and has made us with marks of personality to be persons too.

We can understand something of His compassion because we too have a tiny measure of compassion. We can understand something of His love because we too have a tiny measure of real love for someone. We can understand some measure of His speaking the truth about history because we too have some small experience of relating a happening in our own history with some small degree of accuracy. We can understand some small measure of disappointment in a spoiled creation because we too have known what a spoiled relationship, or a spoiled garden means to us when we look back with sheer delight at the beginnings. We can understand some small measure of desire to bear pain for another person, to take the burden from someone else, if we have suffered because of loved friends and family members going through physical pain or other frightening experiences. So we have a tiny shred of understanding the titanic love and willingness to suffer for us which God the Father and God the Son knew in planning the way of redemption for lost suffering people.

We do not have a God who is far off, separated from us by such otherness as would be an unbridgeable gulf. We have a God who made us in His own image so that we could relate to Him, and so that such words as "Wonderful, Counselor, The Mighty God, The Everlasting Father, The Prince of Peace" could have enough meaning for us to understand with a sweeping thankfulness. We have enough similarity to the One who made us that when He tells us we are the sheep and He is our Shepherd, we are the bride and He is our Bridegroom, we are the children and He is our Father, we are the branches and He is the Vine we can understand such brilliantly vivid descriptions. He has not written us in an unknown tongue. He has not given us laws, His explanation of as much as we need to know, His unfolding of history in a strange and undecipherable language. He has been careful to use Hebrew, Greek, and syntax and vocabularly that can be translated, and is still being translated, into the languages people use in all nations, kindreds, and tribes, so that it can be understood.

So when we read some more of Psalm 119 together, we read it in a language all of us can understand together. We are not reading a gobbledygook "religious" language. It makes sense. It made sense to the psalmist centuries ago, and it makes sense to us now. We can't exhaust it, but we can get enough out of it to find help for today and to relate to it in our lives right now, and to do something differently than we would have done it otherwise.

> Oh, how I love your law!
> I meditate on it all day long.
> Your commands make me wiser than my enemies,
> for they are ever with me.
> I have more insight than all my teachers,
> for I meditate on your statutes.
> I have more understanding than the elders,
> for I obey your precepts.
> I have kept my feet from every evil path
> so that I might obey your word.
> I have not departed from your laws,
> for you yourself have taught me.
> How sweet are your promises to my taste,
> sweeter than honey to my mouth!
> I gain understanding from your precepts;
> therefore I hate every wrong path.

Your word is a lamp to my feet
  and a light for my path.
I have taken an oath and confirmed it,
  that I will follow your righteous laws.
I have suffered much;
    renew my life, O Lord, according to your word.
      Accept, O Lord, the willing praise of my mouth,
and teach me your laws.

(Psalm 119:97-108)

We can have a Bible in our hands, read, study, meditate, talk to the Lord about it, ask for further understanding, consistently look for help in "doing" rather than just "hearing" His Word. And we can have, whether as children, or as uneducated older people, the possibility of knowing more, understanding more, of what really is truth, what really is right, what really is the answer to Who am I? and What will fulfill me? than any of our brilliant professors who do not love God's law. The democracy of being under God's instruction, being under God's direction, being under God's commandments, being under God's verbalized explanations is a democracy like nothing on earth. Each person can come directly to the Master of the Universe, the King of Kings, the General of Generals and receive an audience.

However, in this democracy we need to continue to ask for discernment. We are living in a rapidly changing age. The moral climate surrounding our children and our children's children is not like the temptations or wickednesses which surrounded those of us who are a bit older. We need to ask for discernment for ourselves, and we need to ask God how we can speak to the next generation in a way which can be understood. We also need to ask how we can live in a way which speaks the same words that our mouths are saying. And it isn't easy. We need to cry out:

It is time for you to act, O Lord,
  your law is being broken.
Because I love your commands
  more than gold, more than pure gold,
and because I consider all your precepts right,
  I hate every wrong path.

(Psalm 119:126-128)

Thank God He is a compassionate God. Thank God that as we study and restudy His law, His instructions, and discover how often and how terribly we have broken His law, not just long ago, but even yesterday, that we can ask for cleansing, not carelessly, but recognizing how much it cost Him and how sorrowful our careless attitudes must make Him. Are we thinking of Christianity as a means of becoming healthy, happy, fulfilled in every material thing, every psychological need, every emotional need, every desire for ease and personal fulfillment right now, in this month, this year, this period of our lifetime in the land of the living? Do we have our hand out for just what we can "get out of it" when we consider living as a Christian? Have we any idea at all of what it means to have become an ambassador representing God (as there are no other representatives right now; angels are not at this period of history being sent down to make truth known)? Do we have any idea of what it means to be a part of the "battle in the heavenlies"? Have we any concept of trying to find out what God's will is hour by hour according to what He has carefully set forth in His Word, the Law, the Bible?

Many people ask, "How can I find God's will?" and so often they are only thinking of this job or that job, this country or that country, this house or that house, a baby now or not, a vacation now or later. Is it wrong to bring small and big decisions to the Lord in prayer asking for His help because we feel great need for it? Of course not. He has clearly told us that if we lack wisdom we are to ask Him for it and He will give us His wisdom, as well as telling us that if we are weak and ask for His strength He can make His strength perfect in weakness. Of course we can ask for all kinds of help and receive it.

But in our desire to know the will of the Lord in small and big decisions, in our desire to not make a big mistake in some of the central decisions of life, we are in danger of missing the boat altogether if at *times* we do not agonize before the Lord with some measure of realizing sometimes we are where David was in Psalm 40 and that we need in our own way to ask for help in knowing and doing God's law. It is always His will for us to be doing His law!

We need to stop rationalizing and skipping over things that we are meant to consider.

As we approach a study of the Ten Commandments, we need to approach it as a time of having the understanding become a part of us in a strong way. Our understanding must be strong enough to cut through the smog that pours out to obliterate their teaching, wherever that smog comes from—in spoken or written word, in music or films, in paintings or other art works, in people's lives or expressed opinions or in preaching.

> Then I said, "Here I am, I have come—
>   it is written about me in the scroll.
> To do your will, O my God, is my desire;
>   your law is within my heart."
> I proclaim righteousness in the great assembly;
>   I do not seal my lips,
>   as you know, O Lord.
> I do not hide your righteousness in my heart;
>   I speak of your faithfulness and salvation.
> I do not conceal your love and your truth
>   from the great assembly.
> Do not withhold your mercy from me, O Lord;
>   may your love and your truth always protect me.
> For troubles without number surround me;
>   my sins have overtaken me, and I cannot see.
> They are more than the hairs of my head,
>   and my heart fails within me.
> Be pleased, O Lord, to save me;
>   O Lord, come quickly to help me. . . .
> You are my help and my deliverer;
>   O my God, do not delay.

(Psalm 40:7-13, 17)

1: The First Commandment

Setting
It had been three months since the children of Israel had come out of Egypt. It had been three months since they had seen the last of the ten plagues which demonstrated to them the power of their God and the vivid difference between Him and the gods of the Egyptians. It had been three months since they had experienced the passover when they had taken the blood of a lamb, family by family or sharing with another family, and put it on the doorposts of their houses. They had been clearly shown the difference between what happened in households where the blood of the lamb was faithfully placed on the doorposts and in those where it was not. The memory of the living firstborn children and animals in contrast to the death of the firstborn in households who had shrugged their shoulders and had scorned the fulfilling of the command God had given through Moses was still fresh in every family. Mothers whose husbands and fathers had fulfilled the command looked lovingly at their firstborn or, if young, hugged him hungrily in their arms. It had been three months since the great cross section of ages, grand-mothers and grandfathers, mothers and fathers, cousins and aunts, racing teen-agers and skipping ten-year-olds, toddlers and babies in arms, had squealed, sighed, sung, laughed as the waters of the

Red Sea rolled back and they wiggled their toes in sheer enjoyment as they walked or ran across the Red Sea.

It had been less than three months since they had joined together in that magnificent blend of voices to sing with Moses:

> The Lord is my strength and my song;
>   he has become my salvation.
> He is my God, and I will praise him,
>   my father's God, and I will exalt him. . . .
> Your right hand, O Lord,
>   was majestic in power.
> Your right hand, O Lord,
>   shattered the enemy. . . .
> Who among the gods is like you, O Lord?
>   Who is like you—
>   majestic in holiness,
>   awesome in glory,
>   working wonders? . . .
> In your unfailing love you will lead
>   the people you have redeemed.
> In your strength you will guide them
>   to your holy dwelling.
>
>   (Exodus 15:2, 6, 11, 13)

It had been less than three months since the time all the crowd of liberated people, liberated from slavery, had stampeded and demonstrated their displeasure and impatience concerning a lack of water. The only water was bitter. They did not sweetly ask the God who had led them and supplied a dry path for them to make this water sweet, but they had grumbled to Moses in no uncertain terms, with apparently no respect or proper fear of the Lord their God. When Moses' cry to the Lord was answered with the giving of a piece of wood, at least some of the grandparents, aunts and uncles, mothers and fathers, teen-agers and small children must have seen that piece of wood thrown into the water, must have been impressed at the miracle of the water becoming immediately sweet and refreshing to quench the thirst of all the people. It was exactly at this time that God gave strong and clear direction, before the commandments were given: "If you listen carefully to the voice of the Lord your God and do what is right in his eyes, if you pay attention to his commands and keep all his decrees, I will not bring on you any of the diseases I brought on the Egyptians, for I am the Lord who heals you."

It was right after hearing these solemn and clear words of warning that hunger began to blot out everything else, and instead of quietly asking for food, loud grumbling and angry blaming of Moses for misleading them broke out from the crowd. Moses made it clear then that any grumbling was not really against him or Aaron. It was against the Lord who had brought them out of Egypt. Having watched the ten plagues and having seen the Red Sea roll back, wouldn't you think they would have been silent?

God let it be known to Moses that a miracle would provide nutritious food. There would be quail that evening. The next morning there would be thin flakes like frost on the ground. It was to be known as manna, and it would continue to be provided for forty years. It was to be gathered six days, morning by morning. Some of the manna was to be preserved miraculously for generations to come to make sure that what God had provided would not be forgotten. So very carefully did God precede the giving of the Ten Commandments with a demonstration of the reality of His existence and His power as Creator of all things that the next lack of water in that thirsty desert land was dramatically provided in a way everyone could see. The elders went with Moses to see closely, but the rock Moses struck was a real rock, and the marvel of what God provided could be seen, felt, heard as any waterfall is heard, as well as tasted and drunk deeply, quenching thirst. It was a dry rock that was struck; it was real water that gushed forth. Just as the majority took part in grumbling and loudly blaming Moses for bringing them out to die of thirst, so everyone took part in seeing, feeling, hearing, and tasting the fresh and amazing water.

The preparation for the giving of the Ten Commandments was a vivid preparation, a vivid demonstration of the existence of God who could act into history, who could hear and respond, and who cared about people and who provided their needs for right then, as well as making promises of a promised land to come.

The reality of what happened immediately before Moses went to meet with God was not something that could be disputed. People's doubts and questions about the reality of the existence of God had ample answer in observable and reassuring evidences. The overwhelming truth of what took place then can only be matched with the overwhelming truth of what is taking place today. People *can* be given answers to their questions, they *can* be certain about the reasonableness of God's existence as Creator and designer of the universe and of human beings made in His image. The problem in Moses' time and in our time is the same: the frightening hardness of heart and the deliberate turning away from the truth of God's existence and of His revelation. Not only did people turn away *from* God, but they turned *to* substitute gods—and they still do. "If only I could see some signs of God's existence," people say today. But they do not differ significantly from those artists, musicians, builders, craftsmen, designers, cooks, agriculturalists, and so on of Moses' time. The children today are not so different, and they are very affected by the example as well as by the teaching of adults, whether in the same family or the next door neighbors.

What did the children and adults hear that day when God called Moses to come up to the top of Mount Sinai? First they heard that He had sent a message to them through Moses saying, "You yourselves have seen what I did to Egypt, and how I carried you on eagles' wings and brought you to myself. Now if you obey me fully and keep my covenant, then out of all nations you will be my treasured possession. Although the whole earth is mine, you will be for me a kingdom of priests and a holy nation."

Can't you imagine an eight-year-old boy and his eleven-year-old sister listening as they silently squeezed each other's hands with excitement? Two little believers, encouraging each other, helping each other as they talked and waited together to see what would come next, thrilled to know that the true living God was going to talk more to Moses, giving messages meant for them all. In contrast to the sheer acceptance of God's Word by two such children, and others whom we know were like this among the adult Levites, were the many who heard and saw but who did not believe. What did they hear next?

"On the morning of the third day there was thunder and lightning, with a thick cloud over the mountain, and a very loud trumpet blast. Everyone in the camp trembled" (Exodus 19:16).

If everyone saw and heard the thunder and trumpet and saw the cloud and lightning and everyone trembled, the difference between the response inwardly and the actions that took place later was the difference between bowing as creature before the Creator and turning away deliberately from Him. No other conclusion can be reached. The inward defiance is a deliberate defiance in spite of the same unfolding of sufficient evidence. "Then Moses led the people out of the camp to meet with God, and they stood at the foot of the mountain. Mount Sinai was covered with smoke, because the Lord descended on it in fire. The smoke billowed up from it like smoke from a furnace, the whole mountain trembled violently, and the sound of the trumpet grew louder and louder. Then Moses spoke and the voice of God answered him" (Exodus 19:17, 18).

It was very, very clear that God was there with Moses. But people in every point of history, convinced of God's existence or not, are mainly concerned with their own immediate comfort or fulfillment and with a removal of anything that annoys or bothers them. People today are the same as those people were at the bottom of Mount Sinai. There are the few who truly want to love God and trust Him and who wait patiently and with expectation for what comes next. We can think of the young brother and sister, climbing to a small foothill to find a flat place where they could watch Mount Sinai as it disappeared into the cloud, to talk seriously while they played a little game with small stones on a bit of level dirt, chewing a few blades of grass growing out of a crevice, waiting with a measure of patience and honest expectation. We can think of other brothers and sisters, too young to be noticed much in their families or communities, believing the truth they have heard and waiting with trust for the next step without the angry grumbling and bitterness which is on every side of them. These are, and were, in the minority.

God had more than the Ten Commandments to give Moses. He had a lot of additional information the people needed, and should have been staggered to receive. Amazing—the God of the Universe, the Creator of all things out of nothing, The Mighty God, the Everlasting Father, was verbalizing that which was to be written down for generations of people. He was making clear how to live in the midst of a frighteningly large number of nations who had false ideas, worshipped false gods, and taught their children lies

about how to live, lies which would mix them up as to Who am I?
and How can I be fulfilled?, distorted patterns which could only
bring agony and frustration, sorrow and complete unhappiness on a
deep level. Amazing—the true living God is now going to reveal
Himself more specifically and clearly. He is going to let people
know how they can live on the basis of who they are and who He is.
He is going to give directions for daily life which will separate these
people from the false, twisted ideas they were poisoned with in
Egypt, ideas that had seeped into their homes in a dense, foglike
penetration. Today the Lord's people, people who call themselves
Christians after His name, claim to have had all their sins washed
in Christ's blood shed in painful sacrifice. But many Christians are
living in the midst of an Egypt with a thousand different faces, an
Egypt with a multitude of false religions and false standards of
living, and false bases of making decisions. People today stand at
the bottom of Mount Sinai with their minds and emotions filled
with egotistical and selfish desires, without waiting to hear what
God requires of them or sets forth as the unchangeable code of
behavior, basis of life, and subject matter for constant meditation,
discussion, and action. One could see that desert of Sinai in all its
dustiness filled with crowds of people shouting, "It's a long time"
and "When is he coming back?" and "Let's *do* something that we
can hear and feel and see and prance around. Let's have some
excitement. I'm tired of waiting and searching. And I'm especially
tired of God's voice of authority. The trumpet was too loud and we
need a leader, anyway, who is right *here*. Who is the nearest and
most likely person to follow? Who will lead us into something
which gives us everything the neighboring people have? How can
we be like everyone else today? We have to relate to the people
around us, we need to *do* some form of the same thing." One could
see the desert in one's imagination peopled with twentieth-century
people, as well as peopled with the people of Moses' time. There
wouldn't be much difference.

Let's go to Exodus 32:1:

> When the people saw that Moses was so long in coming down from the
> mountain, they gathered around Aaron and said, "Come, make us gods
> who will go before us. As for this fellow Moses who brought us up out
> of Egypt, we don't know what has happened to him."

What a shiver should go up our spines. What blasphemy—attributing to Moses what God had done, and then grumbling about it, failing to quote what God had already said to them through Moses, failing to even say the words, let alone trembling to be blatantly acting against them. These were people who had sung the song of Moses with the very tongues and vocal cords that now were acting as if it were perfectly in keeping to sing out a request for other gods! "Oh, Aaron, go ahead and design gods. You've had patterns in Egypt, you know all about other gods." They wanted a mixture of paganism, of practices common all about us, of the denial of God's commands couched in pious words and put into a setting that is supposed to be parallel to worship of the very God both the actions and words are denying. "How could they?" we cry out concerning these Israelites who had had everything happen in just a few months to exhibit to them the truth of God's existence and His faithful leadership, and who were in a time of brief waiting for further communication with Him.

"How long, O Lord, how long?" It is all right to ask that, but *not* to turn aside and say, "Now we'll do our own thing—you've exceeded the limit *we* have put on our waiting." Here are men and women taking the place of God, calling the shots, setting limits on how quickly God must finish what He is doing, or else. How dare they? How dare we? What is going on today in the name of God?

Leadership! So often leadership is the case of a "leader" following the dictates and desires of the people so that he or she can still be a "leader." This kind of "leader" doesn't worry about changing positions over and over again, principles thrown away, "gold earrings melted down" to make any old new code of morals—anything to stay in power! Come to Aaron: "Aaron answered them, "Take off the gold earrings that your wives, your sons and your daughters are wearing, and bring them to me.' So all the people took off their earrings and brought them to Aaron. He took what they handed him and made it into an idol cast in the shape of a calf, fashioning it with a tool. Then they said, 'These are your gods, O Israel, who brought you up out of Egypt.' "

The *name* of the true and living God—placed on a calf made of gold. The *work* of the true and living God—attributed to the calf made of gold.

"When Aaron saw this, he built an altar in front of the calf and announced, 'Tomorrow there will be a festival to the Lord.' So the next day the people rose early and sacrificed burnt offerings and presented fellowship offerings. Afterward they sat down to eat and drink and got up to indulge in revelry."

Now the *worship* of the true and living God is transferred to the calf made of gold!

It follows in quick succession. People want something more to do, to look at, to fellowship in, to see, to taste, to feel, to get emotional about. Hence, they copy the outward things of which false worship is made up, making substitutions for God in certain outward things while still using the language, while still using the word *god*: "these are your gods which brought you up out of Egypt"; "tomorrow there will be a festival to the Lord." Soon the inward transfer is made and all honor is given to another god which is no god at all . . . and finally the worship has turned into an orgy.

Moses was out of sight of the people, and the people were out of Moses' sight, but God saw exactly what they were doing. He also saw into their minds and hearts, their intellectual rationalizing and their emotions, their thinking and their actions. God knew the shift in their base. These people who had been singing with Moses such a short time before, singing of the marvel of the true and living God, had now turned their backs upon Him in a shocking way. Moses had already been given the Ten Commandments. God had written them into the stone; they were readable, legible, understandable. Who was waiting to hear them? I like to think of the little girl and boy, standing aside, talking to each other, encouraging each other not to forget what the true and living God, the Master of the Universe, had already done for them. There was a remnant, there were the Levites, *not* being drawn in to the religious frenzy that was going on. Enough had already been given to them all to make them eager to wait for more from God. God had already said how important it was for them to remember how He had carried them on eagles' wings, and how important it would be to obey Him so that they would be different from all the nations which were following false gods. It was not a matter of ignorance.

The Who am I? and How can I be fulfilled? questions were to be answered by the Creator, who knows who human beings are and what will fulfill their needs because He had made them in His image. He knows the tragic sorrows and the destruction that come from living in the darkness of the lies concerning who people are and what will be fulfilling, as well as living in the darkness of the lies concerning His own existence. Turning away from the truth of God's existence and the truth of how to be in relationship with Him and turning to any one of the numerous false substitutes brings its own devastation to the individual because of the unchangeable fact of who each person is, and who God is. It makes God both sorrowful and angry as well.

Come to Joel a moment and reread what is being taught after a terrible plague of locusts had been followed by drought and famine.

> Hear this, you elders;
>   listen, all who live in the land.
> Has anything like this ever happened in your days
>   or in the days of your forefathers?
> Tell it to your children,
>   and let your children tell it to their children,
>   and their children to the next generation.
> What the locust swarm has left
>   the great locusts have eaten;
> what the great locusts have left
>   the young locusts have eaten;
> what the young locusts have left
>   other locusts have eaten. . . .
> Despair, you farmers,
>   wail, you vine growers;
> grieve for the wheat and the barley,
>   because the harvest of the field is destroyed.
> The vine is dried up
>   and the fig tree is withered;
> the pomegranate, the palm and the apple tree—
>   all the trees of the field—are dried up.
> Surely the joy of people
>   is withered away.
>
> (Joel 1:2, 3, 4, 11, 12)

Joel turns the plight of the drought into spiritual lessons. He speaks of withered joy, of joy and gladness having been cut off, and calls the people to fast and cry out to the Lord. They are not to cry out for better crops and food to fulfill an immediate need, but to recognize how far they had come from truly following the living God.

Jeremiah 9:12-14 explains the kind of destruction that has made Jerusalem a heap of ruins. "What man is wise enough to understand this? Who has been instructed by the Lord and can explain it? Why has the land been ruined and laid waste like a desert that no one can cross? The Lord said, 'It is because they have forsaken my law, which I set before them; they have not obeyed me or followed my law. Instead, they have followed the stubbornness of their hearts; they have followed the Baals, as their fathers taught them.' " Later this chapter speaks of their not being circumcised in their hearts. It is inward stubbornness, the inward turning away from God, always accompanied by a turning to false gods. There is no neutral place. This ninth chapter of Jeremiah comes before the chapter which tells of the idols being like a scarecrow in a melon patch and warns the people of God not to "learn the ways of the nations."

Elders, leaders, Aarons, adults, children—this mass turning away from God, the One and only God, needs to be swiftly interrupted. It is not only a matter of withered joy and frustrated living on a wrong base, but it is a life and death matter. Judgment is necessary, judgment on the correct base, judgment by the true God. It is not kind to let blind leaders go on leading the blind to the edge of a cliff or to the bottom of a volcano!

Up on the mountain, hidden by the cloud, the Lord speaks to Moses: "Go down, because your people, whom you have brought up out of Egypt, have become corrupt. They have been quick to turn away from what I commanded them and have made themselves an idol cast in the shape of a calf. They have bowed down to it and sacrificed to it and have said, 'These are your gods, O Israel, who brought you up out of Egypt.' I have seen these people," the Lord said unto Moses, "and they are a stiff-necked people." God goes on to say that His anger is burning against these people, and says He is going to destroy them so that another nation can be brought forth to take their place. But Moses pleads for them, and asks God not to give the Egyptians occasion to say they were brought out just to be destroyed. His prayer, his intercession, his requests were listened to and answered, and God says He will not destroy them. However, when Moses sees with his own eyes the orgy of false worship and immoral practices going on at their height of frenzy, he properly becomes angry himself and throws the stone tablets with the precious handwriting of God on them, the Ten Commandments, at the foot of Mount Sinai, smashing them in pieces on the ground. Then he took the golden calf, burned it in the fire, ground it into powder, scattered it on the water, and made the people drink it! Aaron answers Moses' angry question as to why he had led the people into such sin by passing the blame on to the people's requests for gods to worship, and says he only melted the gold and, presto! all by itself this calf came out of the fire! Aaron claims a supernatural happening as excuse for his sinful leadership. How familiar in today's scene!

"Moses saw that the people were running wild and . . . [had] become a laughingstock to their enemies." A very important fact of history to remember! Even the enemies who have a false base, who worship false gods and have orgies in front of idols, make fun of those who claim to be the people of the one true God after they fall into the trap of copying them. Even the enemies of God give no sympathy to the people who, claiming to be His people, shift their worship to false methods of worship and put other gods in the place of honor. It may seem strange, but it happened in Moses' time, and it happens today. Christians become the laughingstock of the world at the very time they are trying to conform to the world's way of life and manner of religious practices.

Then comes the confrontation as Moses stands at the entrance to the camp and calls out, "Whoever is for the Lord, come to me." And all the Levites rallied to him. Imagine the reaction of that imaginary little boy and girl who had been so fearful and dismayed by what they saw and heard and felt to be somehow all wrong and upside down. What confusion little children feel when elders, leaders, and their own adult relatives turn away from the truth and begin to act on a false base. It is with this in mind that we must listen to Christ's strong warning in Matthew 18:2-7:

He (Jesus) called a little child and had him stand among them. And he said: "I tell you the truth, unless you change and become like little children, you will never enter the kingdom of heaven. Therefore, whoever humbles himself like this child is the greatest in the kingdom of heaven. And whoever welcomes a little child like this in my name welcomes me. But if anyone causes one of these little ones who believe in me to sin, it would be better for him to have a large millstone hung around his neck and to be drowned in the depths of the sea. Woe to the world because of the things that cause people to sin! Such things must come, but woe to the man through whom they come."

The Israelites' decision to defy God and worship a false god was not something they did only unto themselves. Today, the wrong choices we make concerning what God has said is the way we are to behave toward Him and our fellow human beings result in sins we commit which hurt not only ourselves. All of us are meant to teach and be examples in our actions to the next generation. We are going to be charged with having hurt children by misleading them into sin. We are responsible for our actions and teaching as we affect nieces and nephews, children and grandchildren, neighborhood children, and children in the church. And the more we are known, the more danger there is of widespread harmful leadership to the next generation.

We try to think of what a difference there would have been if the people had waited patiently for the Ten Commandments to be brought to them. They would have welcomed Moses with rejoicing, and Moses would have returned with a thrill to unfold what was written on those tablets of stone. Now time has been horribly wasted, and history has been horribly delayed as well as marred once more. A second trip up that mountain is going to be taken, and Moses will return a second time with the law, to read and explain.

The Lord said to Moses, "Chisel out two stone tablets like the first ones, and I will write on them the words that were on the first tablets, which you broke. Be ready in the morning, and then come up on Mount Sinai. Present yourself to me there on top of the mountain. . . ." Then the Lord came down in the cloud and stood there with him and proclaimed his name, the Lord. And he passed in front of Moses, proclaiming, "The Lord, the Lord, the compassionate and gracious God, slow to anger, abounding in love and faithfulness, maintaining love to thousands, and forgiving wickedness, rebellion and sin. Yet he does not leave the guilty unpunished." (Exodus 34:1, 2, 5-7)

The Lord goes on to talk to Moses and make a covenant verbally with him, saying that He will do wonders, miracles, before the eyes of these people again and again, that they may know He is God indeed. He tells of how He will drive out the nations who worship false gods and teach horrendous false practices of religions connected with these false gods. He says to Moses, "Do not worship any other god, for the Lord, whose name is Jealous, is a jealous God. Be careful not to make a treaty with those who live in the land; for when . . . you choose some of their daughters as wives for your sons and those daughters prostitute themselves to their gods, they will lead your sons to do the same."

When Moses came down from the mountain Sinai with the two tablets of the law in his hands, "he was not aware that his face was radiant because he had spoken with the Lord." At first Aaron and the leaders were afraid to come near him, but soon they did, and he gave them all the commands the Lord had given him on Mount Sinai.

The first commandment should fill us with a proper fear, a deep respect of the Creator, the everlasting God, the infinite-personal God who speaks in a way He expects people made in His image to understand. He identifies Himself and makes clear He exists and that we are to understand that He has acted into history, that He has done things we can know about as well as all the things we cannot expect to know about in our limited finiteness.

And God spoke all these words: "I am the Lord your God, who brought you out of Egypt, out of the land of slavery. You shall have no other gods before me."

God does not say that there are different representations of Himself. In that first commandment He speaks of other gods, of false gods, which His entire Word, the Bible, makes clearly understandable. There is danger of worshiping other gods even when using the name of God, the only God, as the Israelites did with the calf. There is a danger of going through all the motions of worship, with the mind and emotions filled with other things, so that the whole thing is a farce. Religion, as such, is dangerous because it can make people feel they are doing some favor to God by worshiping, by doing some list of things, or not doing a list of other things, when all that they are saying and doing and feeling is in relationship to their own desire to have some sort of peace and prosperity and is directed toward a false god in addition to the bad motive. Wrapping egotistical motives and selfish desires into a bundle of religious fervor is common in many forms of religion and in many forms of worshiping false gods. But such motives are also a danger to those who want to come to the true God, but want to come with no struggle at all about honestly coming to Him with love for Him and a desire to bring Him glory and to please Him.

Come again to Deuteronomy 6: "Hear, O Israel: The Lord our God, the Lord is one. Love the Lord your God with all your heart and with all your soul and with all your strength."

This is what was to be impressed upon the children, to be talked about day and night, on walks and when eating meals and having tea in the garden. "How can we love God more?" How concerned are we about this answer, about a solution to a growing love? God's command, "You shall have no other gods before me," includes the mind, the emotions, the actions day by day, as well as the period of time labeled *worship*.

David calls out in Psalm 18: "I love you, O Lord, my strength . . . my rock, my fortress and my deliverer; my God is my rock, in whom I take refuge." Love is increased by verbalizing it, by enumerating things both mind and emotions can recognize as reasons for love. Cursing God, blaming Him, and doubting His love work in the opposite direction. Human love is spoiled by nasty name-calling adjectives to tear down a person.

We need to recognize that and spend time repairing the damage by showing love in a new way after asking forgiveness and saying, "I'm sorry." We also need to spend time recognizing that our love of God is far from what it should be, first of all, and that we are constantly in danger of putting another god before Him in our concern, attention, time, energy, thoughts, and emotions.

When Jesus was being taunted and heckled by the Pharisees, one of them asked, "Teacher, which is the greatest commandment in the law?" Jesus replied, "Love the Lord your God with all your heart and with all your soul and with all your mind, this is the first and greatest commandment." Jesus' answer makes it even more clear that no other gods are to be loved, that no false god is to creep in and take the place of the wholeheartedness and completeness of our acting in accord with the first commandment. "The most important one," answered Jesus, "is this: 'Hear O Israel, the Lord our God is one Lord. Love the Lord your God with all your heart and with all your soul and with all your *strength.*' "

This first commandment speaks of the existence of a personal God, One who can be loved by us one to one, personally, and One who has made us with a capacity for loving Him, as well as a capacity for loving other human beings. Before all else, we are to love Him, think about Him, do things differently because of His existence, make our conscious choices in the light of His existence. Having no other gods before the true and living God is not an easy command to obey, and when words such as "love with all your heart, with all your mind, and with all your soul and with all your strength" are used, we should feel overwhelmed. Who can do this?

In Romans 3 we are told that the law will silence every mouth! How can we let it search our very beings and not be silenced as to our failures! We have no room for boasting. Paul tells us clearly, however, that after we come to God through faith in Christ, the Lamb who died in our place, taking our punishment, we do not then "nullify the law by this faith . . . Not at all! Rather, we uphold the law."

Because Jesus died for us, to give us a ransom for our sin, to pay the awful price, to take our punishment, does that mean that now we can have other gods before Him? Does that mean we are not meant to love the Lord with all our hearts, with increasing reality and force and depth through the years of our lives? Romans 6:22 says, "But now that you have been set free from sin and have become slaves to God, the benefit you reap leads to holiness, and the result is eternal life." The holiness which is a part of the results, the benefits, which are meant to spill over as the results increase day by day means having no other gods before Him and having our love for Him increase day by day.

Is this stressed in your own life alone before your mirror? Is this stressed in our own lives in our motives for doing this? Is this stressed in our motives for making decisions in our business, hospital, creative work, science, farming, family life, use of time? Is there a practical day by day place on the list in our minds, if not on paper, of carefully weeding out whatever might be encroaching upon God's place in our affections, our worship, our admiration? Is there a danger of our allowing the long list of other gods of the twentieth century—whether of affluence, pride, power, or false religions that are increasing like mushrooms all around us—to infiltrate our own meditation which is a place that belongs to God? How can we meditate on His Word "day and night" if we fill our attention and affection with things that are contrary to His Person, His Law, His Word, His direction to us?

The same passage (Romans 6) that tells us we are not under law but under grace warns and urges us to do something about not letting sin reign, take precedence, have the upper place in our lives. We need to understand sin's nature and that it may be cutting down our growth and healthy development as true Christians.

The first commandment is not to be comfortably shoved under the rug because we are not under law. God forbid! We are to realize that to have other gods before the true God is likened to being a whore. Strong language? This is the language God uses to His people Israel when they enter into false worship of the gods of the nations all around them. It is the language which belongs to anyone putting another god in the place of the one true and living God who alone is to be worshiped, who alone created the world, who is the only One in whose image people were made. In Ezekiel 16 (*King James Version*) the word "whore" is used to describe Israel in the awful religious practices they have entered into with the Assyrians and the Canaanites. In *The New International Version* the word "prostitutes" is used. Listen to verses 30, 31: "How weak-willed you are, declares the Sovereign Lord, when you do all these things, acting like a brazen prostitute! . . . You built your mounds at the head of every street and made your lofty shrines in every public square."

What is God saying? He says powerfully that to give money to other kinds of worship, to build shrines and places of worship which are not given over to the true worship of Himself, is a striking picture of a promiscuous woman. God makes it clear that He considers Israel, the people He has called out and redeemed, His wife. Theirs is a call to unyielding faithfulness. Jesus makes it very clear that all the people of God who are redeemed by looking to the Lamb—both those who for so long looked forward and we who look back—are together His bride. They are to be faithful, faithful as the Bride of Christ waiting for His coming. This is all bound up in the first commandment.

Morning by morning, dinnertime by dinnertime, day-off walk by day-off walk, bedtime reading together by bedtime reading together, special day by the fireside by special day by the fireside—whatever family times we have together, some of the conversation is meant to be in the area of the immediate ways in which we can check up on ourselves. We should also set aside some time to consider ways we could attempt to say the right words, meditate about them, think about them, and do what we are saying.

Take paper and a notebook and write ways in which more attention can be given to God. Write a list of the ways in which love can be worked on, increased, paid attention to. Spending time with someone increases our love, as does spending time among things that person has made. What has God made that has left-over beauty in it, that has not been as badly spoiled as some other things? Don't sit in the sunset worshiping the sun; instead, worship the Maker of the sun! Don't be in danger of worshiping nature; instead, love and appreciate the Creator of the details and the precision of things great and small. Spend time getting out of the concrete and get somewhere (or have someone bring something into your hospital room) where you can see a leaf or a branch, smooth wood with a grain, a bird. Love God as the designer, the artist, the architect of much that you admire, remembering you can't see it yet (you will someday) in all the perfection He made in the beginning.

Talk together and read the variety of things He has given us in His communication, the Bible, and enjoy music He has told us is to be part of our worship. Be sure to have some records of truly great music, if no one is able to make great music in the family. But also be sure to sing and play instruments and clap and bang so that the two-year-olds can make music before the Lord and know that He made them to be able to do so, and to hear and appreciate sounds, because He made us in His image. Talk of the marvelous compassion of God, of how His compassion and love so far surpass ours that we can't imagine how gentle and forgiving He has been, nor how much He has been willing to suffer so that we could one day have perfection forever. Talk about the love of God, in the context of this first commandment. He loved us first!

When you, when we, when our children, when friends question, Why? Why? Why? concerning suffering and affliction and troubles, be sensitive to the fine line that divides grief and sorrow and frustration from bitterness that may be planted as a bad weed to grow and crush out love and worship. Pray for yourself and for all the ones for whom you are responsible, in your own generation, but also in the next generation. Ask for God's help. He alone knows what part of the shock is due to the cause-and-effect history flowing from the fall, and what part is due to a direct attack of Satan, as in Job, and what part is to be used by Him to bring forth someone to a fantastic place of refinement, as silver is refined. So often we do not know the source of our affliction. Pray, communicate, weep before Him, explain to Him that you are confused, ask Him for help in your reactions, actions, words, emotions, and ask that He give His strength in your weakness. Pray that this time may not be wasted, but may bring Satan's defeat, *whatever* part he has, and may bring forth something wonderful to God's glory.

Satan constantly sends his darts against Christians so they may turn to other gods. May we not dabble in anything that even smells of the occult, or of Eastern religions, or of transcendental meditation, or of mixtures of religion with diets or religion with anything that detracts from putting God first, even if it uses Christian language and calls itself Christian. Something else mixed in that may seem innocent in itself can slide into God's first place. *Help me to recognize the danger signals, O Lord. In this twentieth century give me discernment when I turn on the television and courage to turn it right off again. In this twentieth century give me courage to judge what I read, whether in newspapers or books, by your Word. Help me to realize that many things are clamoring to turn my love away from You. Teach me what true fear of You and love of You mean when translated into my everyday life.*

Just as we are to have courage to stay away from false gods, so we are to have courage to take positive action that can be seen so that we naturally are "marked." My husband has written *The Mark of the Christian*. Out of love for God flows love for other people, bringing forth action based on that love. Not putting other gods before the one true God, and truly loving Him with all our hearts and minds and souls and with all our strength is not a passive life of sitting in an ivory tower. It is an active life, as James shows, filled with positive action that has a base. Faith, James tells us, is dead faith if it is not accompanied by action. He tells us that Abraham's "faith and his actions were working together, and his faith was made complete by what he did" (2:22).

Surely our faith in God and in His Word is to be accompanied by action which will show forth our love for Him and which will demonstrate clearly that we are not putting any other gods in His place. Our day-by-day life is not to contradict the truth of the first commandment. We are not to defy the first commandment, nor to treat it lightly. But as we see how easy it would be to break this commandment many times a day in ways we have not yet recognized, we are to understand what is meant by, "all [your] righteous acts are like filthy rags."

Let us thank God for the righteousness of Christ which covers us as a sparkling white linen robe; but let us also be sensitive to the constant danger of subtle shifts in our love. Loving God with all our hearts and souls and minds and strength would fulfill the Who am I? perfectly. I am made with a fantastic capability of love. In that capacity, I can love more than one person at once. The closer I come to loving God in some measure, increasing my love all the time, the more love I can have for my husband, wife, mother, father, aunt, uncle, cousin, friend, neighbor. That love for other human beings becomes like the meal in the barrel and the oil in the cruse of the little widow woman who made Elijah a cake during the famine! There was a famine in the land, but God poured out an endless supply of meal and oil because of this woman's treatment of His true prophet, Elijah.

There is a famine of compassion and unselfish, lasting, growing, true love among human beings because of the blast of egotistic desire to have "rights" protected. In the midst of the famine, however, a true reality of living in the light of the truth of the first commandment would bring an outpouring of an endless supply of love. To love God with all one's heart is not to use up love, but to increase it continually.

2: THE SECOND COMMANDMENT

When the second commandment was read to the people, what a graphic understanding they would have had of its meaning. The little girl and boy would have immediately remembered the look of that golden calf. It did not take education nor long experience to recognize the stark fact that all who had taken part in prancing around the golden calf with the name of God on it, and in doing various religious antics they had seen the Egyptians do in their Apis-bull worship and other kinds of idolatry had already done what was being forbidden.

The reading of the second commandment did not come in a vacuum. It came to people who had bowed down to a golden calf made out of their own jewelry. It came to people whose ears still rang with their own voices singing Moses' gorgeous song of praise to the living God as they sang in their drunken orgy to the golden calf. They wouldn't have had a problem about whether or not something made by men's hands for the tabernacle, when commanded by God, was a denial of this commandment. They knew very well the difference between admiring the beauty of an art work which they had in their own tapestries and jewelry, the hangings of their own tents, that which they would later make by God's command for the tabernacle, and an idol, made for the specific purpose of representing a god to worship. There had been two kinds of things in their experience before. So when the commandment was read aloud, it should have caused great shame and great humiliation with desire for forgiveness; it should not have caused any kind of confusion.

The first commandment had to do with God's *being*, His existence, His place in the whole of the universe and in all of time as the one and only God. Only God is the Creator; all else is created. The first commandment establishes the fact that there is no other God. All others called by the word *god* are false.

The second commandment deals with the worship of God as contrasted with the worship of false gods. God, who has made human beings, knows that the answer to Who am I? and How can I be fulfilled? includes a need to bow in worship to Himself. We have a *need* to worship the Creator as well as a capacity to worship Him. We have a *need* to love the Father in heaven who has made us as well as a capacity to love Him. To be living without this fulfillment is to be unfulfilled indeed.

Because we are human beings made with these capacities, to turn away from the true God, to reject Him, to ignore Him, to rebel against the true God does not leave anyone in a vacuum of neutrality. There is also a turning to, an accepting of, an attempt to obey someone else in His place—a false god, an idol. This was true when Moses was on Mount Sinai receiving the Ten Commandments; it was true many times in Old Testament history; it has been true at every turn of history; and it is true today. It has never been more true than today.

Many twentieth-century people are turning away from God with great superiority and pride. The turning to a terrific variety of idols and false gods, old and new man-made religions, is amazing in this period of "modern" men and women. People feel liberated when they turn from God the Creator and His laws, even while they are allowing handcuffs to be put on their wrists as they become bound in Satan worship, Eastern religions, cults with a great diversity of origins, occult practices, and now a deluge of women goddesses restored from Greek times, and added to by modern inventions of new goddesses. Our universities are a hotbed of "sophisticated" new religions, even though they are only old pagan idol worship dressed in new purple. Many old practices such as abortion and infanticide, once thought of as a part of pagan religions and acceptable only to people who worshiped idols made by men's hands, have now come back in a flood. The turning *away* from God is always a turning *to* replacements. The marvel of real worship and the true emotion it brings forth is substituted by frenzy and whipped-up emotion.

Bob Dylan is right when he sings,

> You gotta serve somebody
> You gotta serve somebody
> It may be the Devil or it may be the Lord
> But you gotta serve somebody.

Moses stood there that day at the bottom of the mountain, among the dry rocks and dusty ground, surrounded by tents and the press of people, eager and intense children among them, as well as crying babies and bleating lambs, and read forth the next commandment in a strong voice, strong with deep emotion as to its intense importance in the light of what *is*, what is true and what is false. I am sure he felt restraint, but only enough restraint to be able to read. He must have still been angry enough to give an edge to his voice. These people had been worshiping their earrings— melted down, to be sure; but how disgusting that they had prostituted the emotions that had belonged to God alone, and replaced exalted and uplifting worship to the true God with gross and banal religiosity to a false god, an idol in the shape of an animal. Moses' message was God's Word, not his own.

He read:

"You shall not make for yourself an idol in the form of anything in heaven above or on the earth beneath or in the waters below. You shall not bow down to them or worship them; for I, the Lord your God, am a jealous God, punishing the children for the sin of the fathers to the third and fourth generation of those who hate me, but showing love to thousands who love me and keep my commandments." (Exodus 20:4-6)

In Leviticus 19:4 the Lord told Moses to speak to the entire assembly of people, Israel, and to say to them, among other laws: "Do not turn to idols or make gods of cast metal for yourselves. I am the Lord your God." Later in that same chapter, in verse 31, God says, "Do not turn to mediums or seek out spiritists, for you will be defiled by them. I am the Lord your God."

Don't you see that added to turning away from loving God and worshiping Him is the turning away from going *to* Him for help? Human beings cannot get along without seeking advice, help, counsel, wisdom, direction, because in this fallen world, where so many things go wrong, they need to turn to "someone higher." The only One higher is God in His perfect wisdom, might, power, knowledge, and love. People need to turn to God for help. God says, "Ask of me" over and over again. But many do not listen. They turn instead to idols and mediums and spiritists, to all manner of promised supernatural help, outside of God. Now such help can be pure fake, given for some kind of gain, or it can be supernatural. However, if it is supernatural, it is not God who is being called on, and there is no supernatural "neutral" person or persons to whom to go. If one is not going to the true and living God for help from what is called "the other world," one is going to the devil or demons. Turning away from God is turning to the kind of help God has long warned people about. When Eve and Adam turned away from God's counsel concerning the fruit, they turned to Lucifer's counsel and followed it. "You'll be like gods"—a tempting counsel. Advice or counsel is often followed by a result. The course of history for centuries has been changed by individuals and nations who have followed advice from the enemies of God and of true truth.

Isaiah says it so beautifully in his poetic writing, which is a part of God's Word to us in the Bible:

> Woe to those who go down to Egypt for help,
>   who rely on horses,
> who trust in the multitude of their chariots
>   and the great strength of their horsemen,
> but do not look to the Holy One of Israel,
>   or seek help from the Lord.

(Isaiah 31:1)

The 20th Psalm speaks to us in the same vein:

> May the Lord answer you when you are in distress;
>   may the name of the God of Jacob protect you. . . .

> Some trust in chariots and some in horses,
>> but we trust in the name of the Lord our God.
>>> (verses 1, 7)

What is being talked about here is not the use of war equipment. It is a strong combination of the negative warning and the positive command. We are to go to the true and living God for help and put our trust in *Him*. We are not to turn away from Him to idols, or false gods, or the ones who are behind the false gods. We are not to bow down to them. We are not to ask help from them. It would be like going to an enemy terrorist army to get protection from the enemy. In the illustrations that fairy stories give us, it would be like the chicken putting her trust in the wolf for protection, and believing his lies of seduction. Any child should be able to understand this—as with so much of what God makes known to people.

When I was a little girl my mother would often say to me, "Edith, I know just who you've been playing with today." She knew because I had become something like the other little girl, whichever one it was, enough like her that the girl could be identified by my changed accent, my mannerisms, and other telltale changes. Children often copy other children quite unconsciously. So do adults. We are affected by the people we spend time with, in one way or another. God makes clear to us that not only is it sin to bow down to idols and worship or serve them, but that there is an effect which follows very definitely. People who worship idols become like them. Sometimes it is possible to identify someone's religion or philosophy just by the look of that person, as well as by the actions and conversation.

Psalm 115 points this out beautifully in verses 1 to 11, and urges trust in the Lord.

> Not to us, O Lord, not to us
>> but to your name be the glory,
>> because of your love and faithfulness.
> Why do the nations say,
>> "Where is their God?"
> Our God is in heaven;
>> he does whatever pleases him.
> But their idols are silver and gold,
>> made by the hands of men.

They have mouths, but cannot speak,
eyes, but they cannot see;
they have ears, but cannot hear,
noses, but they cannot smell;
they have hands, but cannot feel,
feet, but they cannot walk;
nor can they utter a sound with their throats.
Those who make them will be like them,
and so will all who trust in them.
O house of Israel, trust in the Lord—
he is their help and shield.
O house of Aaron, trust in the Lord—
he is their help and shield.
You who fear him, trust in the Lord—
he is their help and shield.

What a call this is to turn *away* from idols and *to* the Lord who alone is able to help and to be a protection! Yet the world is so full of people who are behaving with deceit and violence, hate and selfishness. Today's newspapers give us ample illustrations of how utterly people, century after century, have become like the idols they trust. It is not necessary to go to far-off tribes for examples; our cities and increasingly widespread areas of our own country are full of such examples. The call to obey the second commandment is not a call to something that has no meaning in the twentieth century. Human beings who pattern themselves after false gods or false concepts about who they are give false patterns to the next generation. This occurs in every area of life until even the basic concept of what a mother or father is, what a family is, what a boy or girl is, is twisted and bent like a piece of faulty metal.

Elijah lived in such a day as ours. People then who should have known the true living God, and to whom Elijah prophesied, were worshiping Baal instead. God had not sent rain on the land for three years, and when King Ahab met Elijah he blamed the lack of rain on Elijah. "Are you the troubler of Israel?" asks Ahab. Elijah replies: "I have not made trouble for Israel. But you and your father's family have. You have abandoned the Lord's commands and have followed Baals. Now summon the people from all over Israel to meet me on Mount Carmel. And bring the four hundred and fifty prophets of Baal and the four hundred prophets of Asherah, who eat at Jezebel's table." "So Ahab sent word throughout all Israel and assembled the prophets on Mount Carmel. Elijah went before the people and said, 'How long will you waver between two opinions? If the Lord is God, follow him; but if Baal is God, follow him.' "

It is impossible to mix the worship of false gods, of idols, with the worship of the one true God. There cannot be a synthesis, a blurring of the two diametrically opposite things. The absolute truth of God's existence and person cannot be mixed with the relative potpourri of false gods. The one true God is not one among many. He is One alone—three Persons, but only one God. Indeed we need to say to many people who are confused and muddled about truth, "How long will you waver between two opinions?"

That day Elijah, who was the only prophet of God left, confronted the 450 prophets of Baal. He told them to get two bulls. One the prophets of Baal were to prepare, and one Elijah would prepare. They would place them on two altars, put wood on the altars, and then call upon their god, while Elijah called upon the name of the Lord. Whichever one answered by sending fire, "he is God," Elijah said. Then all the people said, "What you say is good."

Do you remember the history of what happened? After the prophets of Baal had prepared their bull on the altar, they called on Baal from morning till noon, but there was no response, no one answered. Do remember that Elijah taunted them and told them to call louder because perhaps their god was asleep! So they not only shrieked louder but cut themselves with knives, as was their custom. Nothing happened.

In the evening Elijah called everyone to come to him. He then prepared an altar with the wood and bull upon it. He poured water over the wood as well as in a trench around the altar. Three times he got the men to soak it all with water. Then he prayed: "O Lord, God of Abraham, Isaac and Israel, let it be known today that you are God in Israel and that I am your servant and have done all these things at your command. Answer me, O Lord, answer me, so these people will know that you, O Lord, are God, and that you are turning their hearts back again."

"Then the fire of the Lord fell and burned up the sacrifice, the wood, the stones and the soil, and also licked up the water in the trench. When all the people saw this, they fell prostrate and cried, 'The Lord, he is God! The Lord—he is God!' "

Notice: when people turn away from idols and turn to God, it is a complete turning *from* the false *to* the true. There has to be a complete turning *away*, as well as a turning *to*. The danger today, as in any other day in history, is an attempt to hold on to something of false worship, of idols, of meditating in an Eastern way, of sitting crosslegged in partial adoration of the sun, of some false way of getting help in making decisions through fortune-tellers or astrology.

Sometimes in biblical history the false prophets were not so clearly outside, calling on a contrasting name in a way that a confrontation could take place outside the temple. In Ezekiel 9 there is a description which also could apply to our own day. This description is of the temple, the Lord's house, being full of idolatry. This was a vision that Ezekiel had, but it is frighteningly close to what we can observe in our own time of history.

> He said to me, "Son of man, have you seen what the elders of the house of Israel are doing in the darkness, each at the shrine of his own idol? They say, 'The Lord does not see us; the Lord has forsaken the land.' " (8:12)

> He then brought me into the inner court of the house of the Lord, and there at the entrance to the temple, between the portico and the altar, were about twenty-five men. With their backs toward the temple of the Lord and their faces toward the east, they were bowing down to the sun in the east. (verse 16)

God speaks of these things as detestable, an outward appearance of being His people, but bowing before a variety of idols when they think He does not see!

But there is more than this that is condemned. There is the matter of an inward idol, an "idol set up within hearts" that Ezekiel identifies. "Thou shalt not turn to idols" is speaking also of an inward turning.

The warning that applies here is that although Man looks on outward appearances, God looks on the heart. Outwardly a person may seem to be believing and conforming to Christianity, but inwardly he may be "setting up idols in his heart," as is spoken of in Ezekiel 14.

> Some of the elders of Israel came to me and sat down in front of me. Then the word of the Lord came to me: "Son of man, these men have set up idols in their hearts and put wicked stumbling blocks before their faces. Should I let them inquire of me at all? . . . Therefore say to the house of Israel, 'This is what the Sovereign Lord says: Repent! Turn from your idols and renounce all your detestable practices.' " (vv. 1-3, 6)

There are a variety of idols—things which take the place of God, things that push aside all thought of putting God's laws first, or conforming to the Bible's teaching—which people have set up in their hearts. We need to be aware of this danger, and not take one small list of sinful things which are not our own temptations and point our fingers at others without recognizing our own danger. There needs to be a turning away from and a turning to. We must turn away from idols, whatever they may be, and turn toward God, asking for help to be *real* and not false inwardly. Remember, Nehemiah confessed the sins of Israel and the fact that they had not obeyed God's commandments and asked for forgiveness before he could begin the work of rebuilding the broken-down wall of Jerusalem at that time.

First John 1:5—2:2 is a help to us when we discover that we have been guilty of bowing down inwardly or outwardly to one or another kind of idol, and blatantly breaking the second commandment even while declaring in one way or another that we are believers, people of God, Christians.

> This is the message we have heard from him and declare to you: God is light; in him there is no darkness at all. If we claim to have fellowship with him yet walk in the darkness, we lie and do not live by the truth. But if we walk in the light, as he is in the light, we have fellowship with one another, and the blood of Jesus, his Son, purifies us from every sin. If we claim to be without sin, we deceive ourselves and the truth is not in us. If we confess our sins, he is faithful and just to forgive us our sins and purify us from all unrighteousness. If we claim we have not sinned, we make him out to be a liar and his word has no place in our lives. My dear children, I write this to you so that you will not sin. But if anybody

does sin, we have one who speaks to the Father in our defense—Jesus Christ, the Righteous One. He is the atoning sacrifice for our sins, and not only for ours but also for the sins of the whole world.

The passage goes on to say that we know that we have come to know Him if we obey His commands. And it also says that a person is a liar if he says he knows Him but does not do what He commands.

Frightening? It is solemn and serious. To be flippant about being a Christian as if it were a thing of outwardly sticking up one's hand in a meeting, with no inward turning away from—and turning to—and recognition of some of the sin that is present and needs confession to the Lord, to go on day after day with no change taking place as walking in the light replaces walking in the dark is to be in a frightening place indeed. It is marvelous to know the truth of the effectiveness of Christ's death in washing away our sins. This same Word of God, however, tells us to be conscious of the battle that is taking place as Satan tries to tempt us in one way or another to stop trusting God, to turn away from Him. The end of 1 John 5:21 is, "Dear children, keep yourselves from idols." This comes directly after verse 20 which tells us that the Son of God has come and has given us understanding so that we may know Him who is *true*, right after telling us that the world is in control of the evil one. Satan is not yet vanquished, the battle rages, and we are being utterly stupid if we do not realize that it is an active battle. Therefore, John admonishes us, "Dear children, keep yourselves from idols." We can't take for granted that we will. We need to ask daily for the Lord's help both in recognizing where the danger lies, and in turning away from the pitfall.

In Ezekiel 13 we have another facet of the whole situation as it continues in one period of intensity or another. Here we discover that one of the great dangers is being confronted by false prophets, "foolish prophets who follow their own spirit and have seen nothing. . . . They say, 'The Lord declares,' when the Lord has not sent them. . . . They lead my people astray, saying, 'Peace,' when there is no peace, and because, when a flimsy wall is built, they cover it with whitewash."

Jeremiah, quoting the Lord, speaks of these false prophets too, in 23:16-18:

"Do not listen to what the prophets are prophesying to you;
    they fill you with false hopes.
They speak visions from their own minds,
    not from the mouth of the Lord.
They keep saying to those who despise me,
    'The Lord says: You will have peace.'
And to all who follow the stubbornness of their hearts
    they say, 'No harm will come to you.'
But which of them has stood in the council of the Lord
    to see or to hear his word?
Who has listened and heard his word?"

Jeremiah is warning with an urgency which God placed upon him when God told him he was to speak to everyone He sent him to. You remember Jeremiah felt inadequate and said he was only a child and couldn't speak, and God promised to put His words in Jeremiah's mouth. These *are* God's words of warning. It is possible to be led by false prophets who claim to be giving a message from God, but who are filling people with false hopes. To lull people into a comfortable stupor when danger is upon them, to lead people to the edge of a cliff telling them there is no cliff there, is simply another form of turning them away from God to the "scarecrow in the melon patch."

In Ezekiel 34 God speaks to such leaders in these words, "Woe to the shepherds of Israel who only take care of themselves! Should not the shepherds take care of the flock?"

Shepherds who should be caring for people so that they are well taught and well prepared to stand against all the onslaught of pressure to be like the culture around them are often the very ones that have so let down in their own lives and messages that they are now in the state that Israel was in when Jeremiah proclaimed what God's judgment was going to be: "You have as many gods as you have towns, O Judah; and the altars you have set up to burn incense to that shameful god Baal are as many as the streets of Jerusalem" (Jeremiah 11:13).

In the New Testament, warnings were given to us from Israel's history. In case you think we are now so strong that we do not need any warning, we can be absolutely sure that is a dangerous "think." My mother would have said to me, "You have another think coming!" Listen to 1 Corinthians 10:1-21. Part of this passage needs to be reread in connection with another one or two of the commandments, but it should be set in full context here as we consider the danger of idolatry and false worship of other gods.

> For I do not want you to be ignorant of the fact, brothers, that our forefathers were all under the cloud and that they all passed through the sea. They were all baptized into Moses in the cloud and in the sea. They all ate the same spiritual food and drank the same spiritual drink; for they drank from the spiritual rock that accompanied them, and that rock was Christ. Nevertheless, God was not pleased with most of them; their bodies were scattered over the desert. Now these things occurred as examples, to keep us from setting our hearts on evil things as they did. Do not be idolaters, as some of them were; as it is written: "The people sat down to eat and drink and got up to indulge in pagan revelry." We should not commit sexual immorality, as some of them did—and in one day twenty-three thousand of them died. We should not test the Lord, as some of them did—and were killed by snakes. And do not grumble, as some of them did—and were killed by the destroying angel. These things happened to them as examples and were written down as warnings for us, on whom the fulfillment of the ages has come. So, if you think you are standing firm, be careful that you don't fall! No temptation has seized you except what is common to man. And God is faithful; he will not let you be tempted beyond what you can bear. But when you are tempted, he will also provide a way out so that you can stand up under it. Therefore, my dear friends, flee from idolatry. I speak to sensible people; judge for yourselves what I say. Is not the cup of thanksgiving for which we give thanks a participation in the blood of Christ? And is not the bread that we break a participation in the body of Christ? Because there is one loaf, we who are many, are one body, for we all partake of the one loaf. Consider the people of Israel: Do not those who eat the sacrifices participate in the altar? Do I mean then that a sacrifice offered to an idol is anything, or that an idol is anything? No, but the sacrifices of pagans are offered to demons, not to God, and I do not want you to be participants with demons. You cannot drink the cup of the Lord and the cup of demons too; you cannot have a part in both the Lord's table and the table of demons. Are we trying to arouse the Lord's jealousy? Are we stronger than he?

The temptation just to try this or that, or to go along with some false worship because of embarrassment from having been unexpectedly involved in a dinner engagement at someone's home, is sometimes a very strong one. Does it matter? It does. True, the idol is just a Buddha made of ivory or bronze or soapstone, or the idol is just an old Indian relic, and the incense is just a sweet-smelling smoke, and the bit of smoking that may go along with it can be passed quickly by, or the ceremonial cup being passed isn't after all "anything"—but the worship involved is exactly what Satan is trying to get you, to get me, to get any of us involved in. And he is real, and his army of demons is real, waiting to laugh in God's face about what some of His people have done, people who claim to be His and have just bowed to one of the gods, or idols, or symbols representing him, Satan. Satan's temptations continue to be the same through the ages, and his great drive for as long as he has is to destroy and spoil anything he can of God's creation, God's created people, and God's relationship with His people.

Remember Jesus as he was tempted by the devil after fasting for forty days and forty nights in the desert. One of the temptations was exactly that of bowing, just for a moment, to a false god, with a very attractive result attached. Of course, as always with Satan's promises, the result would have turned to disaster, and not one of us would have had eternal life had Jesus not stood firm and turned away from Satan. Listen:

> Again, the devil took him to a very high mountain and showed him all the kingdoms of the world and their splendor. "All this I will give you," he said, "if you will bow down and worship me." Jesus said to him, "Away from me, Satan! For it is written: 'Worship the Lord your God, and serve him only!' " Then the devil left him, and angels came and attended him. (Matt. 4:8-11)

When someone asks you to "just try out the Ouija board," *remember to turn away*. When someone asks you to join in in a new kind of religious worship "just for this evening," when you are suddenly caught in a very bad situation which you know is not a game but is tied in with idols or false gods, remember what we are told in Hebrews 4:14-16:

> Therefore, since we have a great high priest who has gone through the heavens, Jesus the Son of God, let us hold firmly to the faith we profess. For we do not have a high priest who is unable to sympathize with our weaknesses, but we have one who has been tempted in every

way, just as we are—yet without sin. Let us then approach the throne
of grace with confidence, so that we may receive mercy and find grace
to help us in our time of need.

Now is the time to remember this "life-saving rope" being
thrown to us! Right now, when on this university campus the girls
are drawing you in to "just see" the worship of the goddesses, and
the great high priestess is someone you know, and the temptation
to see what it is all like and to go barefooted and barebreasted along
with the rest of them for the pagan worship out in the sunshine or
moonlight with the tempting words, "it's only another kind of enjoying nature" is ringing in your ears—now is the time to remember that Jesus especially pointed out that He had been tempted to
bow before the devil, and He, Jesus, invites you to come in His
name to the throne of God and ask for help in running away in the
other direction.

Don't forget: when you run *away,* you also run *to.* When you run
away from the false gods, there is Someone waiting to receive you.
"Come unto me." Remember that invitation when you are being
laughed at, taunted, pulled in the other direction. This invitation
to come *to* the throne of grace is especially connected with the fact
that Jesus has gone through that *same* temptation and therefore
that He will understand.

It isn't just the new feminist goddess worship that may suddenly
come into your back yard; there are so many varieties of Eastern
cults which come into contact with you through diet and nutrition
books, or when the whole group suddenly urges you to sit with
them on the sand at Carmel to meditate on the sun. It is all too easy
to rationalize and think, "They may be worshiping the sun, but I
can sit in the same position with them and pray to the true God."
This is nothing but rationalization, and it occurs all too often.

In Korea some years ago, Christian churches and groups were
told they had to bow at the Shinto shrine. A Shinto shrine could be
put in a Christian church, just in a corner, and if the congregation
bowed to the shrine first, then they could go on and have their
other worship. This is exactly what the early church faced—the
exclusiveness of worshiping God through the Lord Jesus Christ
rather than including worship of other gods. Some American missionaries and some Koreans compromised and bowed. Other

young Koreans were cruelly tortured to make them bow, yet died rather than bow. They "held firmly to the faith they possessed." They acted upon their belief that the Bible speaks truth and that it is wrong to bow to idols, or to false gods in any form. They paid a terrific price for their loyalty to the living God and joined the other martyrs who are waiting for the glorious moment of the resurrection. At that day we will discover just what the special martyr's crown consists of! One thing we may know: the comparison between what the martyrs died for and the results following the attempt to synthesize light and darkness by trying to bow before the true God with an addition of a few idols and false gods on the side would be too titanic to put into human words!

Habbakuk the prophet gives the contrast as vividly as any description in the Bible:

> "Of what value is an idol, since a man has carved it?
>   Or an image that teaches lies?
> For he who makes it trusts in his own creation;
>   he makes idols that cannot speak.
> Woe to him who says to wood, 'Come to life!'
>   Or to lifeless stone, 'Wake up!'
> Can it give guidance?
>   It is covered with gold and silver;
>   there is no breath in it.
> But the Lord is in his holy temple;
>   let all the earth be silent before him."

(2:18-20)

Our turning away from any form of idols, and our spending true reverent silence before the Lord, leaves neither time nor place for a "collection of curios" which are in fact idols to the people who made them and in the countries in which we bought them. With all the travel going on today, many Christians think it is a fascinating hobby to collect carvings which are not just art works (art works, or arts and crafts type carvings, are, of course, very different and a good thing to possess or to be interested in). There are idols, or copies of idols, which are a part of horrible heathen worship of a variety of gods. To decorate a shelf in your home with these or other things used in false worship makes a foolish mixture in the atmosphere of your home. It opens the possibility for something far

more dangerous. One should have a healthy respect for the powers
of darkness. The early Christians in the Book of Acts took seriously
the need to rid their homes of all that they had which had been
connected with their former practice of sorcery. They brought
their scrolls together and burned them publicly (Acts 19:19). One
might say the scrolls were just parchment. But the men knew there
was more than this to it. There was an uproar in Ephesus because
the silversmiths felt they were going to lose their trade—the making of shrines to the goddess Artemis. Purely economic gain was
their interest then, and that kind of interest in pushing drugs as a
sacrament, trinkets, copies of idols, Buddhas, and other things
connected with false worship keeps a pressure on weak people in
the twentieth century too.

The gaining of money in exchange for the dragging down of souls
has been a part of each period of history, and our moment is no
better. Such things should not be penetrating Christian homes.
Our homes should have an atmosphere which leads to a freedom,
both inwardly and outwardly, to worship and communicate with
the true and only God, without hindrances.

In this context we should remember 2 Corinthians 6:15, 16,
although we may want to reread this entire passage in light of
another commandment. "What harmony is there between Christ
and Belial? What does a believer have in common with an unbeliever? What agreement is there between the temple of God and
idols? For we are the temple of the living God. As God has said, 'I
will live with them and walk among them, and I will be their God,
and they will be my people.' "

Old homes, new homes, tiny cottages, magnificent palaces, little
huts, big tents, a sleeping bag on a wanderer's back, or a trailer—
whatever the home of the believer, the astonishing and breathtaking promise is that God will live with us, and walk with us, and will
be our God, and we will be His people. How very, very appropriate is the next sentence we read as we turn away from all forms of
other gods and idols, as we prepare our homes and our walks to be
visited by such a One: "Since we have these promises, dear
friends, let us purify ourselves from everything that contaminates
body and spirit, perfecting holiness out of reverence for God" (2
Cor. 7:1).

Rather than putting anything at all in His place in our lives, rather than asking what benefits we can get out of being a Christian, our own question should be, how can *we* properly reverence Him and bring joy to Him.

3: THE THIRD COMMANDMENT

How many people take part in some worship of God week after week, reading, chanting or singing the Psalms? Over and over again, as in Psalm 111, they say the words, "I will extol the Lord with all my heart." In that psalm the Lord is extolled for His works, His deeds, His righteousness, His wonders or miracles, His provision of food and other basic needs of life, His provision of redemption. Then, "holy and awesome is his name. The fear of the Lord is the beginning of wisdom; all who follow his precepts have good understanding. To him belongs eternal praise."

In Psalm 115 they read or sing, "Not to us, O Lord, not to us but to your name be the glory, because of your love and faithfulness." How many times do the words flow from thousands of throats in chorus, as well as alone, "The cords of death entangled me, the anguish of the grave came upon me; I was overcome by trouble and sorrow. Then I called on the *name* of the Lord: 'O Lord, save me!' " (Psalm 116:3, 4).

How many people in the world are at least outwardly making a gesture of worship in repeating what is called the Lord's prayer? You remember that Jesus was teaching crowds of people on a mountainside and that we have been given the content of that teaching. It has been preserved for us in the Bible. In the midst of all this teaching (and we will consider more of this sermon of Jesus in another chapter) came this: "Our Father in Heaven, hallowed be your name. . ." What a tremendous declaration to make to God, in prayer, as a request. "Hallowed be your name." Come now to Isaiah 57: "For this is what the high and lofty One says—he who lives forever, whose *name* is holy: 'I live in a high and holy place, but also with him who is contrite and lowly in spirit, to revive the spirit of the lowly and to revive the heart of the contrite' " (v. 15). For centuries people have been told by the prophets that God's name is holy, and have been reminded in a variety of ways of that third commandment. Then when Jesus said, "this is how you should pray," the use of God's name, "Our Father who art in heaven," is followed by that request, "hallowed be thy name."

What is the third commandment?

The *King James Version* gives it: "Thou shalt not take the name of the Lord thy God in vain; for the Lord will not hold him guiltless that taketh his name in vain" (Exodus 20:7). It is given in Leviticus again in this way in the *King James*, 19:12, "And ye shall not swear by my name falsely, neither shalt thou profane the name of thy God: I am the Lord." The *New International Version* gives us more insight into the original language. Exodus 20:7—"You shall not misuse the name of the Lord your God, for the Lord will not hold anyone guiltless who misuses his name."

All those people, many of whom had been shouting the name of God in front of the golden calf, are listening to Moses read the law. Think of our imaginary little brother and sister. What chills and shivers would go over them as they heard this solemn and strong pronouncement coming from God! "Ooooooh," we can hear them say, "to put God's *name* on a calf, to worship as the Egyptians did and only use the *name* of God. *What* a misuse that was!"

Each person in each century who hears the Ten Commandments should shiver with recognition of how they apply to something very close, something we have done, I have done, you have done, in one way or another. What are the ways we have misused the name of God? What are the ways people are constantly tempted to misuse the name of God? This name which is to be so reverently feared, honored, respected, and loved, this name which Jeremiah 10:6 says is mighty in power—this is the same name which God explained to Moses, and through Moses to us, as unchangeable forever.

Remember that Moses has approached the burning bush, and God has told him to take off his shoes because the very ground is holy with God's presence. God speaks to Moses in an audible voice, in a language Moses understands, with vocabulary that is not too difficult to translate. Moses asks God questions. One principal question is about God's name. He is afraid that the Israelites will be all mixed up because of all the idols and false gods of the Egyptians. His question is one of identification. How could he identify the one true God to the children of Israel?

> Moses said to God, "Suppose I go to the Israelites and say to them, 'The God of your fathers has sent me to you,' and they ask me, 'What is his name?' Then what shall I tell them?" God said to Moses, "I am who I am. This is what you are to say to the Israelites: 'I AM has sent me to you.'" God also said to Moses, "Say to the Israelites, 'The Lord, the God of your fathers—the God of Abraham, the God of Isaac and the God of Jacob—has sent me to you.' This is my name forever, the name by which I am to be remembered from generation to generation." (Exodus 3:13-15)

God's name was identified, set apart from all other gods, from all false idols, to be the same from generation to generation. Any confusion about the true and living God, the Creator of the Universe, the One who walked and talked with Adam and Eve and who talked to Moses in the burning bush, was to be straightened out by identification: His name was the same.

"I AM has sent me to you." He exists, He has existed, He will always exist. There is no other. His identity was to be known in just that simple declaration of His name.

Come down now many generations later to a group of Israelites asking questions in no gentle fashion, taunting Jesus. There were the other Israelites who were His disciples and who loved Him and followed Him. These who are asking questions are a different group. Jesus has just said that if a man keeps His word, he will never see death. And the unbelieving Jews let out a stream of objections ending with, "Who do you think you are?"

Jesus replied, "If I glorify myself, my glory means nothing. My Father, whom you claim as your God, is the one who glorifies me. Though you do not know him, I know him. If I said I did not, I would be a liar like you, but I do know him and keep his word. Your father Abraham rejoiced at the thought of seeing my day; he saw it and was glad."

"You are not yet fifty years old," the Jews said to him, "and you have seen Abraham!"

"I tell you the truth," Jesus answered, "before Abraham was born, I am!" (John 8:54-58)

It was then the Jews picked up stones to stone Jesus, but he slipped away and hid from them, easily away and out of sight, as it was not time for him to die. Why stone him? Because if Jesus was not God, He would have misused the holy name of identification which God gave to Moses. The name I AM was to identify God so that the children of Israel could have complete confidence to go out of Egypt into the wilderness. They would *know* by that name, or could know, or should have known, that they were following a leader that the living God had sent.

Jesus never broke one of the Ten Commandments, and we know He did not misuse the name of God in any way. The name I AM rightfully belonged to Him.

Jesus was not leading anyone astray by using the identifying name of God. He was speaking truth. It should have been clear to those who had handed down from generation to generation all that Moses told them to hand down. It should have been clear to people who had had conversation and discussion in the morning, at breakfast, at lunch, during an afternoon walk, at supper, in the evening. It should have been clear to those who, day after day, kept alive the memory of the law, as well as of the wonders God had performed, God who had appeared to Moses in the burning bush and had said that His name was I AM. Any family that had followed God's commands to "tell your children and your children's children" would have been prepared for this very moment of history when the Messiah would come and say, "I tell you the truth, before Abraham was born, I AM."

I AM means then that the present tense applies, has applied, will apply forever. And in identifying the one true living God, part of that identification must indicate that He is everlasting. John 1:1,

2, 3, 14 helps us to see that this I AM applies to Jesus to make clear that He is God and has always been "there."

> In the beginning was the Word, and the Word was with God, and the Word was God. He was with God in the beginning. Through him all things were made; without him nothing was made that has been made. In him was life, and that life was the light of men. The light shines in the darkness, but the darkness has not understood it.

> The Word became flesh and lived for a while among us. We have seen his glory, the glory of the one and only Son, who came from the Father, full of grace and truth. John testifies concerning him. He cries out, saying, "This was he of whom I said, 'He who comes after me has surpassed me because he was before me.'" From the fullness of his grace we have all received one blessing after another. For the law was given through Moses; grace and truth came through Jesus Christ. No one has ever seen God, but God the only Son, who is at the Father's side, has made him known.

No, when Jesus made known the fact that He is I AM, He was not breaking the third commandment, but fulfilling it. And although the mystery of the Trinity can never be fully understood by any one of us, yet we *can* know that Jesus came with the identifying name, which made clear not only that He was the long promised Messiah, but that He was the Creator: "Through him all things were made." Yet He was a separate Person, the Son, who could be in communication through prayer. A mystery? Yes, but a mystery clearly spoken about, and made known to us as fully as we are able to comprehend it.

The next day John the Baptist identified Jesus as the Messiah so long looked forward to in all the times of sacrifice of the little lambs, looked forward to by Abraham and Isaac on Mount Moriah, and by so many thousands through the centuries: "Look, the Lamb of God, who takes away the sin of the world!"

The holy names of God are only to be applied to the Father and to the Son and to the Holy Spirit. The misuse of the names of God is a serious thing, as serious at any time of history, and the only way of forgiveness is through the Lamb, whose compassion, along with the compassion of the Father and the Holy Spirit, has opened the possibility of being forgiven.

Before going on to some ways this third commandment may be
broken without people being aware of the seriousness of what they
are doing, let's go to the last book of the Bible, the book of Revelation, to find a marvelous clarification of I AM. Here the glorified
Christ comes to talk with John and show him things he is to write
down for us, these centuries later, and for all those who lived in
between. God is so gentle and loving in the magnificent way He
cares for us! He wants us to know as much as we can about what we
are waiting for. He could have left us completely without anything
to read and meditate on, as well as without anything to cheer us up
as we see the sadness and violence and troubles all around us, as
we suffer pain and disappointment. But He didn't leave us. He
gave us comfort, and hope, and a glorious peek through the curtains at some of what we are going to see that day when the curtains
rise, the music bursts forth, the trumpet sounds, and we have
some tiny idea of what is being ushered in!

I will quote only small bits, but we need to be aware of the
continuity of the importance of the name of God, of that which
alone belongs to God.

> Look, he is coming with the clouds, and every eye will see him, even
> those who pierced him; and all the peoples of the earth will mourn
> because of him. So shall it be! Amen. "I am the Alpha and the Omega,"
> says the Lord God, "who is, and who was, and who is to come, the
> Almighty." . . . On the Lord's Day I was in the Spirit, and I heard
> behind me a loud voice like a trumpet, which said, "Write on a scroll
> what you see. . . ." I turned around to see the voice that was speaking
> to me. And when I turned I saw . . . (read that great description about
> the Son of Man's glory) . . . Then he placed his right hand on me and
> said: "Do not be afraid, I am the First and the Last. I am the Living
> One; I was dead and behold I am alive for ever and ever! And I hold
> the keys of death and Hades." (Revelation 1:7, 8, 10-12, 17-19)

> "Holy, holy, holy
> is the Lord God Almighty,
> who was, and is, and is to come."

Whenever the living creatures give glory, honor and thanks to him
who sits on the throne and who lives for ever and ever, the twenty-four
elders fall down before him who sits on the throne, and worship him
who lives for ever and ever. They lay their crowns before the throne
and say:

"You are worthy, our Lord and God,
   to receive glory and honor and power,
for you created all things,
   and by your will they were created
   and have their being."

(Revelation 4:8-11)

No one will misuse the name of the Lord, the name of God, the name of the Lamb, in heaven. Perfect reverence and glory and honor will be given to the Creator by those of His created beings who will be with Him forever and ever there. But the fantastic thing is that during all eternity the "I AM," the "who was and is and is to come," will still have meaning. Time will not be wiped out, but its extent will have more meaning and fill us with more awe concerning the Alpha and Omega who had no beginning and will have no end . . . more awe than we can imagine now!

How dare we not study to find out what the misuse of God's name right now may consist of?

In Revelation 15 there is a gorgeous picture of a sea of glass mixed with fire, the likes of which you and I have only seen at sunset in some amazing seaside place. Beside this sea in heaven stand all those who have been victorious over Satan, singing the Song of Moses and the Lamb. In that song they are talking about the name, that name which is not to be misused now and which is still to be praised then.

"Great and marvelous are your deeds,
   Lord God Almighty.
Just and true are your ways,
   King of the ages.
Who will not fear you, O Lord,
   And bring glory to your name?
For you alone are holy.
All nations will come
   and worship before you,
For your righteous acts have been revealed."

(Revelation 15:3, 4)

In chapter 21 of Revelation, when John sees the new heaven and the new earth, he tells of the One who was seated on the throne saying, "It is done. I am the Alpha and the Omega, the Beginning and the End."

In Revelation 22:12-14, 16, 17 it seems clear that it is Jesus speaking to John for him to write for us: "Behold, I am coming soon! My reward is with me, and I will give to everyone according to what he has done. I am the Alpha and the Omega, the First and the Last, the Beginning and the End. Blessed are those who wash their robes, that they may have the right to the tree of life and may go through the gates into the city. . . . I, Jesus, have sent my angel to give you this testimony for the churches. I am the Root and the Offspring of David, and the bright Morning Star. The Spirit and the Bride say, 'Come!' And let him who hears say, 'Come!' Whoever is thirsty, let him come; and whoever wishes, let him take of the free gift of the water of life."

A tremendous invitation!—given by the One who died to make it possible to invite people in this way. But do not forget that all through the Word of God, right up to the very end, the seriousness of glorifying, honoring, respecting, treating as really holy the name of God is stressed over and over and over again. We can have no excuse. We can't say, "Oh, I didn't know it meant *that*."

What then does the third commandment mean today? What should the third commandment mean daily, to me and to you?

Perhaps the first thing that comes to your mind is cursing and swearing and using vulgar language in combination with names belonging only to God. In school, at work, in walking along the street, in watching television or movies, in reading any kind of newspaper or magazine or book, the name of God used to curse events or human beings or circumstances or disappointments is a common sound in our ears. The recognition of this as blasphemy is not difficult. The realization that God's name, or God's creation, or God's attributes are being misused, taken in vain, or blasphemed should be renewed consciously. We should not take it for granted as being all right. We should not slip into unconscious usage of it just because we live in an alien world, among fellow workers, neighbors, schoolmates, who follow other gods. For them, such use of the name of God is a part of their daily vocabulary, used for emphasis.

This kind of misuse does need recognition and should be consciously worked on. That is, if a blasphemous adjective comes to mind, it is an important thing to substitute a very different adjective which does not misuse God's name in any way. Language becomes a very poor and limited thing of expressing ideas and thoughts, of telling incidents or stories, if the vocabulary is not being constantly enriched with accurate words to give emphasis, without falling back on the shock element of curses.

There are many other ways, however, to misuse God's name, and some of these are very seldom pointed out. Hence, many who would be horrified at the thought of cursing or swearing are in danger of breaking the third commandment.

There is a misuse of human beings' names which is criminal and punishable by law. If a person carefully practices another person's signature and signs it to a check, and thereby gets money from the other person's bank account, this is called forgery, as well as stealing. Forgery is a criminal act in the eyes of the law. To use another person's name and to say that this is your right is to steal not only their money if that name is affixed to a check or a money order, but it is to steal their reputation.

To say, "Susan told me to tell you. . . ." or "Prisca asked me to say that she said . . ." or "John told me to ask you to give money to buy this field . . ." if indeed there is no clear evidence for any such message is to use forgery to get other people to make choices or decisions or take actions which would not otherwise have been made or done. Whatever ways there are to misuse a name, forgery is one of the worst.

How often do people forge God's name to a request, or an order, or a promise, or a message of some kind? It is a serious thing to say, "God told me you were to *give* this," or "God told me you were to *do* that," or "God told me I should come and give you this message" unless it is absolutely certain that the command, the request, the message came from God. There is too frequently a very light and easy use of the phrase, "God told me" when the ideas have come from a person's own mind and have not at all been revelations from God. The use of God's name, as if one had a signed note from Him, is a very serious thing to attach to a request one is making of someone else to do something in one area or another of Christian work. A claim to have the right to use God's name in this way can be a serious forgery. To claim to know exactly what God wants another person to do is to usurp the place of the Holy Spirit who is meant to lead the people of God, the sheep of the Shepherd, the believers, individually.

It is extremely easy to put blots on other people's reputations by misrepresenting them. It is much worse to misrepresent God, to decide what His messages and directions are to other people in practical and specific things such as the use of time, money, talents, energy, possessions, and so on. To double-check ourselves we need to stop and ask, "Is this a forgery? Or is this really something that has come from God?" God's signature is on the Bible, His Word. We need to pray daily that we be kept from temptation, kept from the temptation to forge His signature in a way that would be a terrible misuse of His name. It is not a light thing to use God's name, even if it seems to be a "spiritual" use of His name. To use God's name to back up one's own ideas, or to use His name in exercising authority over other people who should be coming directly to Him themselves, is a breaking of the commandment not to misuse His name.

In Ezekiel 13 we have an account of false prophets who, even though they are not prophesying in the name of false gods and idols, but in the name of the true God, are not saying anything which comes from Him at all.

The word of the Lord came to me: "Son of man, prophesy against the prophets of Israel who are now prophesying. Say to those who prophesy out of their own imagination: 'Hear the word of the Lord! This is what the Sovereign Lord says: Woe to the foolish prophets who follow their own spirit and have seen nothing! Your prophets, O Israel, are like jackals among ruins. You have not gone up to the breaks in the wall to repair it for the house of Israel so that it will stand firm in the battle on the day of the Lord. Their visions are false and their divinations a lie. They say, "The Lord declares," when the Lord has not sent them; yet they expect their words to be fulfilled. Have you not seen false visions and uttered lying divinations when you say, "The Lord declares," though I have not spoken?

" 'Therefore this is what the Sovereign Lord says: Because of your false words and lying visions, I am against you, declares the Sovereign Lord. My hand will be against the prophets who see false visions and utter lying divinations. They will not belong to the council of my people or be listed in the records of the house of Israel, nor will they enter the land of Israel. Then you will know that I am Sovereign Lord.

" 'Because they lead my people astray, saying, "Peace," when there is no peace, and because, when a flimsy wall is built, they cover it with whitewash, therefore tell those who cover it with whitewash that it is going to fall. Rain will come in torrents, and I will send hailstones hurtling down, and violent winds will burst forth. When the wall collapses, will people not ask you, "Where is the whitewash you covered it with?" ' "

God spoke strongly against these self-appointed prophets of Israel. He condemned them for acting as if their own imaginings were coming from God. False prophecies like these deceive people so that they live in a false sense of peace.

There are also other ways of breaking this commandment. In the book of Jude we are warned of what was happening then and will keep happening, a warning of "godless men" who have "slipped in among you." This warning is a reference to the turning away which has taken place throughout all history, which has been mixed up with the false naming of the name of God. "Woe to them! They have taken the way of Cain; they have rushed for profit into Balaam's error; they have been destroyed in Korah's rebellion. These men are blemishes at your feasts, eating with you without the slightest qualm—shepherds who only feed themselves. They are clouds without rain, blown along by the wind; autumn trees, without fruit and uprooted—twice dead."

To name the name of God can be a terrible breaking of the third commandment: "You shall not misuse the name of the Lord your God." We have not been aware of the need to be careful how we use the name of God. We have not realized what an act of forgery it is to tack the name of God and the outward forms of worship onto what may be described as "clouds without rain," or as "autumn trees, without fruit and uprooted." What a bleak picture! But how terrifying to think that when the world, given over to false gods or idols, looks at people who name the name of the true living God, and who are labeled his ambassadors, they often see just such empty clouds and uprooted fruitless trees. This is certainly a misuse of God's holy name.

Years ago someone very close to me was working for a big denominational mission board. Though not a Christian at that time, this girl was a skillful writer and had among her other work various articles to be included in the mission magazine month by month. She often wondered whether her writings, which were written completely from a Marxist viewpoint, would be deleted from the magazine, but the editor liked her stuff very much, and only cautioned from time to time, "Be sure to put enough 'Lord' in it to satisfy the evangelicals."

At the time of the Presbyterian General Assembly when Dr. G. Gresham Machen was being tried and put out of the denomination, a Greek scholar who stood for the truth of the New Testament and the whole Bible, the girl writer I mentioned heard a speaker, a prominent church leader, come into a back room after his message and stridently ask the staff who had heard him on the loud speaker, "Well, did I put enough 'Lord' in it to satisfy all the little old ladies?"

Let's go back to Exodus 20:7 again and reread the third commandment. "You shall not misuse the name of the Lord your God, for the Lord will not hold anyone guiltless who misuses his name."

To use the name of the Lord to "satisfy little old ladies" or to "satisfy the evangelicals" can in no way be called anything but a misuse of His precious and holy name. The same lips that pray "Hallowed be thy name" render that declaration meaningless when they go on to talk about using the name of the Lord to fool people as to the content of articles, sermons, or lectures. The only comparison I can think of is the use of the word "democratic" sprinkled liberally in names of rallies and seminars for communistic teaching. The use of words to convey an opposite meaning to what the speaker really is saying is one of the worst forms of deceit. To do that with the name of the Lord is to slander Him in a shocking way.

God punished Moses because he and Aaron took credit for bringing water out of the rock. God had told him to speak to the rock before the eyes of the Israelites (Numbers 20:9-12), and rather than quietly speaking so that the Israelites would know that God was performing a miracle for them, we are told:

> He [Moses] and Aaron gathered the assembly together in front of the rock and Moses said to them, "Listen, you rebels, must we bring you water out of this rock?" Then Moses raised his arm and struck the rock twice with his staff. Water gushed out, and the community and their livestock drank. But the Lord said to Moses and Aaron, "Because you

did not trust in me enough to honor me as holy in the sight of the Israelites, you will not bring this community into the land I gave them."

Taking credit for what the Lord is doing, putting one's own name on another person's work, is another way of misusing the Lord's name.

To take someone else's painting, statue, or short story and to sign your own name and put it in a competition as your own is plagiarism. It may sound opposite, but it ends up the same—the misuse of a name. The correct name is being tossed in a waste-basket, or obliterated by ink eraser, and another name substituted. It is the correct name that is being misused when the work, be-longing to the person of that name, is attributed to someone else. The honor and praise belonging to the person who really did the work is given to another who did not do it! The appreciation is given to the wrong person. The family of the artist who is wronged when his or her work is plagiarized becomes indignant, upset, frustrated when people will not believe that the name attached to the work is wrong, and that their beloved father is really the creator of the work in display.

The people to whom the living God, the Master of the Universe, the Creator of heaven and earth, is their Heavenly Father, should be incensed when His work and all His creation is attributed to other names. God's name is wiped out, deleted, erased from His creation in a diversity of ways, and the credit, the praise, the explanation of the work is given another name. All who love God, all those who are His children through the Messiah, should realize that God's name is being misused. This transfer of the name of God should be something we are sensitive to, not a thing to be taken for granted without any inward reaction at all, or any emotion.

We need to actively resist a shrug of the shoulders and a flat unresponsive feeling when all creation is attributed to other causes and the name of the Creator is entirely left out. We need to read and reread such passages as these:

> "To whom will you compare me?
>   or who is my equal?" says the Holy One
> Lift your eyes and look to the heavens:
>   Who created all these?

He who brings out the starry host one by one,
    and calls them each by name.
Because of his great power and mighty strength,
    not one of them is missing. (Isaiah 40:25, 26)

"I am the Lord; that is my name!
    I will not give my glory to another
    or my praise to idols." (Isaiah 42:8)

To give God's praise to *chance* and to declare that everything we know in the world and the universe came by accident is to sign "chance" to all of God's creation. It is an insult to His name as much as it would be an insult to Bach's music, or Michelangelo's statues to sign "chance" where the name of the composer or artist should be. It isn't that we need to make a loud noise during a lecture at school, or get up and object to the university professor, thus interrupting his every sentence, but we should react publicly in some way, when it seems the opportune moment. But whether we speak publicly or not, we need to have a private time, after hearing lectures, reading articles, seeing films, reading books which credit another cause for God's creating and upholding the universe, during which we follow the admonition in Psalm 95:6, 7.

Come, let us bow down in worship,
    let us kneel before the Lord our Maker;
for he is our God
    and we are the people of his pasture,
    the flock under his care.

And again in Psalm 96:8, 9—

Ascribe to the Lord the glory due his name;
    bring an offering and come into his courts.
Worship the Lord in the splendor of his holiness;
    tremble before him, all the earth.

There needs to be an active proper use of the Lord's name, an unashamed honoring of Him, in addition to not misusing His name in any of the blatant ways. However, even in praising God there is danger of rendering lip service only, an outward display of praise and worship which has nothing real inside to back it up. This is another form of misusing the Lord's name which each of us needs to check up on.

We can misuse the Lord's name by saying over and over again, "Praise the Lord, hallelujah, praise the Lord," while in our minds we are planning our menus for the day, or figuring out how much the taxes are going to be, or looking at a neighbor and thinking what a pain in the neck he is, or feeling we simply can't take another illness in the house, and we have just heard that Johnny is being sent home from school with the mumps. The words can be on the lips with sound coming from the throat, but the mind can be totally occupied with other things, full of ideas to make more money or to get a better price for the old car by painting it up, thoughts so very far from the words coming out that they have no connection.

If our mouths are expressing devotion to the Lord by merely repeating words over and over again with no real thought or involvement of the whole person, then we are in danger of misusing the name of the Lord. We are in danger of vain repetition, of babbling like pagans, if we repeat words without honestly thinking of what we are saying. When we say, "I love you," or praise each other in a horizontal relationship, if it is to mean anything real to the other person we give some reasons for why we think that person is wonderful or special or kind or thoughtful, and our communication has some verbalized expression of thankfulness as we relate something the other person has done.

Imagine coming to your father in the back garden after he has just weeded the rose garden, trimmed the bushes, cut the grass, made a lovely sharp line around the lawn so that it looks like a park and saying to him, "Praise dad, praise dad, praise dad!" There is so much to praise him for and he would be made happy by your telling him, "I really appreciate the beauty of this place you have landscaped and now have done so much work on. The grass looks fantastic with that sharp line, and the roses are wonderful since the weeds are gone. You really are a great gardener."

Imagine coming home to find a beautiful table set with a rough beige linen cloth, a bowl of daisies in the center with a rock and moss making a flower arrangement of the bowl, with white candles lit and a steaming basket of homemade rolls on the table and the wonderful fragrance of a roast chicken and apple pie mingling as it comes from the kitchen, and saying, "Praise mother, praise mother, praise mother." How much more she would like you to notice the details of her artistic creation of a table setting, and to remark that no one can make apple pie like hers!

True praise of the Lord starts first within the person. It should be with all the heart, with all the mind, and with all the soul, just like the love we are meant to have for the Lord. No, we can't be perfect, but we are meant to attempt to be real, solid, not just a thin layer that peels off like a veneer table that buckles and ripples the first time you put a hot teapot on it. We are meant to love and praise the Lord with thankful hearts, minds full of thoughts of the marvel of who He is, and what He has done, and of the wonderful promises He has given. To praise Him takes some care and thought, which is far deeper than the mouth or the throat.

The negative concern to not misuse the name of the Lord does not imply a vacuum. Even if we could become suddenly perfect and never misuse the name of the Lord again in this life, we are called upon to use His name in a positive way as we grow in our relationship with Him.

How, practically, can we begin to be conscious day by day of what it means to not misuse the name of the Lord and to grow in our proper honoring of His name? The three areas are always involved—our thoughts, our words, our deeds, or put another way, our meditation, our verbalizing to other people, and our actions. The whole person is involved.

If we think the third commandment does not matter now that our sins have been forgiven and we have been cleansed by the blood of Christ, we have not understood the practical directions the New Testament gives for a Christian life. Each thing we do is meant to be done to the glory of God, to the praise of His name, to represent His holiness and love in some small and partial way, because we are the only ambassadors He has placed in the world at this time. Ours is not a schizophrenic life. We are not meant to live a Jekyll and Hyde existence.

Come to Colossians 3. After explicitly listing sinful things that are to be "put off," "put out" of our lives, including slander and filthy language, then comes the positive admonition, to be read and reread, over and over again. We need a daily reminder from God's Word as to what our standards are.

Therefore, as God's chosen people, holy and dearly loved, clothe your-selves with compassion, kindness, humility, gentleness and patience. Bear with each other and forgive whatever grievances you may have against one another. Forgive as the Lord forgave you. And over all these virtues put on love, which binds them all together in perfect unity. . . . And whatever you do, whether in word or deed, do it all in the *name* of the Lord Jesus, giving thanks to God the Father through him. (Colossians 3:12-14, 17)

The test of whether or not we are real is not an outward thing. Remember in the Old Testament God speaks of circumcision being not real unless it is the circumcision of the heart. In other words, it is the true belief and honest worship of God, the inward thankful-ness for His love and provision of salvation, the attitude of heart when calling upon His name, that counts to God. The reality of what is going on inwardly then comes out in the very mundane things of life, not in the repetition of empty declarations.

Jesus gives us a picture of the future in Matthew 25 which helps us to realize how we can bring honor and glory and joy to the Lord in very amazing and unseen ways.

"Then the King will say . . . 'Come, you who are blessed by my Father; take your inheritance, the kingdom prepared for you since the creation of the world. For I was hungry and you gave me something to eat, I was thirsty and you gave me something to drink, I was a stranger and you invited me in, I needed clothes and you clothed me, I was sick and you looked after me, I was in prison and you came to visit me.' " (Matthew 25:34-36)

And when the people asked what all this meant, when they did all that for Jesus, for the Lord, the answer was given: "I tell you the truth, whatever you did for one of these brothers of mine, you did for me" (Matthew 25:40).

How can we fill the gap left by not misusing the name of the Lord? By reading His Word, the Bible, to discover how to be solid all the way through, to not be frivolous Christians wanting to use God's name for what we can get out of it. By discovering the need to do all that we do honestly in His name, as we put the bedpan under feeble old grandmother, as we mix up a hot milk drink for little Giandy who is sick for the sixth time in a row and bring it with a smile and a story to read, as we buy an outfit for a pregnant girl and tuck in all the vitamins she needs along with a bunch of flowers to encourage her, when we take a basket of groceries plus a nutbread we baked ourselves for the family whose dad left and mother can't get a job because of her twins, as we do these things with an inward, silent, secret talking to the Lord telling Him, "I'm doing this because of the compassion I have which You have given me, along with Your strength; but thank You for telling me that at the same time I can be doing it all directly for You in Your name."

Jesus has said that His name could be used to ask, to make requests in prayer to the Heavenly Father. Just as we spoke of the horrible danger of falsely saying, "God told me" and thereby forging God's name, so we need to be careful in prayer to come remembering the cost, the price paid, the seriousness of the death of Christ, which opened the way for us into the Father's presence because of the name of Jesus.

We may be thankful that in the light of our calling to "purify ourselves from everything that contaminates body and spirit, perfecting holiness out of reverence for God" (2 Corinthians 7:1), we indeed may ask for help from God Himself. He is waiting for us to ask for help in not misusing His name. He has promised to give us His wisdom when we realize that we lack wisdom and stop to honestly ask for it. He has promised to give us His strength in our weakness, when we ask for that. And we have been promised the help of the indwelling Holy Spirit when we ask for His help too. The marvel of the Lord's commands is that He does give us a way, not only of forgiveness, but of going on to grow. I wonder what would happen if every Christian, considering all the places and ways in which he or she had been misusing the name of God, prayed for forgiveness and then asked God's help in Jesus' name to do what Paul calls upon us to do: "Let us purify ourselves from everything that contaminates body and spirit, perfecting holiness out of reverence for God."

4: THE FOURTH COMMANDMENT

We are told that it was on the fifteenth day of the second month after the children of Israel had come out of Egypt, about six weeks out in the Desert of Sin, which is between Elim and Sinai, that the grumbling about food began. "If only we had stayed in Egypt where we had pots of food, all we wanted. Now, Moses, you've brought us out here to die."

You can imagine them, old and young, fat and thin, pregnant mothers and big brothers and sisters, cousins and grandparents, grumbling and murmuring together. Imagine the young brother and sister we pictured before, listening, wondering, talking about how the God who had rolled back the sea so fantastically might do something about their hunger. Think of these two representing the minority among the majority, who kept quiet and had some expectant feelings within themselves that perhaps they didn't talk about. Perhaps a tiny expectant minority. The fact that the people differed in their responses is clearly shown by what happened next.

> Then the Lord said to Moses, "I will rain down bread from heaven for you. The people are to go out each day and gather enough for that day. In this way I will test them and see whether they will follow my instructions. On the sixth day they are to prepare what they bring in, and that is to be twice as much as they gather on other days." (Exodus 16:4, 5)

Then Moses went and talked to all the people and told them they had not really been grumbling against Aaron and himself, but against God. Moses also said that they would know it was the Lord when they would soon find meat in the evening, and all the bread they could eat in the morning, because the Lord had heard their grumbling.

Moses told Aaron to call the entire Israelite community together. While Aaron was talking to them about coming before the Lord, they looked toward the desert and saw the glory of the Lord appearing in the cloud. What a clear piece of evidence the whole community had as they saw something which must have been more glorious than the most beautiful sunrise or sunset! It was then that Moses heard the Lord tell him definitely that there would be meat at twilight and that in the morning they would all be able to gather bread. Our compassionate and patient God, who had already brought these people across the Red Sea and had rescued them from slavery, now says, "Then you will know that I am the Lord your God" (Exodus 16:12b).

What an exciting demonstration! What a practical piece of evidence! Here was something that could be smelled, tasted, digested for a balanced nourishment, handled with an interest to discover a new texture. Here was a new kind of food, proof that God existed, proof that He had heard their grumbling—not a very respectful prayer, but they had made a kind of request in a nasty way; they would remember that, it had just taken place—and that He had cared to answer. Was there a unanimous flood of feeling? Did everyone respond in the same way? Was there an awe, reverence, and desire to do exactly as God instructed them to do?

We are given explicit evidence for the diversity of response. It is not that people had different amounts of evidence—they all had the same opportunity to know, to believe and carry out instructions.

What happened? Read it straight from the Bible (Exodus 16:13-30).

That evening quail came and covered the camp, and in the morning there was a layer of dew around the camp. When the dew was gone, thin flakes like frost on the ground appeared on the desert floor. When the Israelites saw it, they said to each other, "What is it?" For they did not know what it was. Moses said to them, "It is the bread the Lord has given you to eat. This is what the Lord has commanded: 'Each one is to gather as much as he needs. Take an omer for each person you have in your tent.' " [An omer is probably about two quarts or two liters.] The Israelites did as they were told; some gathered much, some little. And when they measured it by the omer, he who gathered much did not have too much, and he who gathered little did not have too little. Each one gathered as much as he needed.

Then Moses said to them, "No one is to keep any of it until morning." However, some of them paid no attention to Moses; they kept part of it until morning, but it was full of maggots and began to smell. So Moses was angry with them.

Each morning everyone gathered as much as he needed, and when the sun grew hot, it melted away. On the sixth day, they gathered twice as much—two omers for each person—and the leaders of the community came and reported this to Moses. He said to them, "This is what the Lord commanded: 'Tomorrow is to be a day of rest, a holy Sabbath to the Lord. So bake what you want to bake and boil what you want to boil. Save whatever is left and keep it until morning.' " So they saved it until morning, as Moses commanded, and it did not stink or get maggots in it. "Eat it today," Moses said, "because today is a Sabbath to the Lord. You will not find any of it on the ground today. Six days you are to gather it, but on the seventh day, the Sabbath, there will not be any."

Nevertheless, some of the people went out on the seventh day to gather it, but they found none. Then the Lord said to Moses, "How long will you refuse to keep my commands and my instructions? Bear in mind that the Lord has given you the Sabbath; that is why on the sixth day he gives you bread for two days. Everyone is to stay where he is on the seventh day; no one is to go out." So the people rested on the seventh day.

What a wonderful *first* teaching about the one day out of seven. "Bear in mind that the Lord has given you the Sabbath." The first thing the Lord made known to the whole community of Israelites concerning this day, this one different day a week, was that it was a gift! It was God's gift to the people He had made in His own image, people who were to work, to be creative, to do a variety of things— till the land, make tapestries, care for sheep, cut wool and make thread to weave cloth, make musical instruments and play music on them, plant vineyards and orchards, make furniture from wood and bowls and baskets from reeds and rushes. Human beings who could work hard at a great diversity of exciting things needed a proportion of *rest*.

God made it clear when He gave them the manna—which, after all, was not such hard work to collect and boil or bake, but which nevertheless was a consistent work to be done day by day—that He was giving a gift to them, a day of rest. If someone wanted to gather manna only every other day, it did not work—the manna went bad, stunk, had horrible little white maggots in it just over one night. But because God wanted the people to have a rest, He made it possible to have one day a week, Friday, be a day when twice as much could be gathered, and the next day could be a day of simply eating and resting, enjoying a time of refreshment, a time of replenishing the weariness that came from six days' work.

The God who made people, who knows the answer to Who am I?, has made it clear that one answer is, "I am a person who needs one very different day in seven, a day of rest." One answer to What will fulfill my needs? is that one day in seven, one seventh of my time, as a human being, needs to be spent in not doing all the same things as are done on all the other days.

The people of Israel had discovered over and over again, week after week, that it did not work when they tried to cheat by gathering more than one day's supply of manna, and that it also did not work if they went out to gather on the seventh day what they had not stored up on the sixth day. The people of Israel had had time enough to find out what a day of rest was like. I am sure that in Egypt slaves were not given a day off. Slaves, who were beaten to make more bricks out of less material, who were treated harshly, did not have a six-day work week! This new schedule was indeed a gift which would have been noticed, and certainly some would have discussed the benefits.

I like to think of our little girl and boy sitting quietly together on the Sabbath, eating their loaves made from the manna, watching the clouds scudding by in the sky, listening to the birds, finding a special feeling of awe as they discussed together how amazing it was that there was something different about the Friday manna. Certainly some sensitive ones had thanked God and worshiped Him in their hearts with more reality. Certainly some sensitive people had come to feel greater love for the thoughtfulness of their

God, whom Moses had been telling them about, because He had provided a rest day for them—even while others started to take it for granted.

All this had been taking place for at least six weeks, as it was the third month after leaving Egypt that they arrived at Sinai. All this had been a careful and practical background for hearing and understanding the reading of the fourth commandment. It did *not* come in a vacuum.

> "Remember the Sabbath day by keeping it holy. Six days you shall labor and do all your work, but the seventh day is a Sabbath to the Lord your God. On it you shall not do any work, neither you, nor your son or daughter, nor your manservant or maidservant, nor your animals, nor the alien within your gates. For in six days the Lord made the heavens and the earth, the sea, and all that is in them, but he rested on the seventh day. Therefore the Lord blessed the Sabbath day and made it holy." (Exodus 20:8-11)

Remember that this is the fourth commandment. The first is to love God with all one's heart and mind and soul; the second is the strong warning not to turn to other gods or idols, not to mix up any other false worship with the worship of the one true God; the third points out the serious attention to be given to not misusing the name of God in *any* way. Now comes the giving of a special day for rest and for worship, a day for contemplating how one has served God during the week, a day when we are freed from other responsibilities to have time to emphasize loving God, turning completely away from any compromise with false gods and idols, respecting His name. This one day in seven is to help the person take that day to have time to review these first three commandments and to consider whether he or she has been faithful or not, rather than being so diverted by increasing work that there is no time for reflection.

The first four commandments all have to do with our relationship with God.

The last six commandments all have to do with our relationship to other human beings.

To answer the questions Who am I? and What will fulfill me? the commandments help us understand the truth about reality, help us see the base upon which human beings can operate at their fullest capacity—physically, emotionally, psychologically, intellectually, spiritually. The reason the commands are so strongly hedged about with warnings and strong contrasts as to what happens when they are kept or broken is that people so quickly turned away from the true and living God to follow all sorts of horrible and false gods, even to the extent of burning their own babies as sacrifices. They were also denying the reality of who they themselves were, insuring lives of being misfits, trying to be something they were not made to be.

This is one of the basic truths that people do not know today! People, with their twisted ideas of the universe, have come to accept that they are machines. People, with their counterfeit gods and idols, their egocentric demands to have their rights, their total misunderstanding of who they are and what will fulfill them, have come to look for fulfillment in caricatures, in nonexistent beings. People today not only do not *know* what a human being is and needs for daily fulfillment, but they don't know what a man is, a woman is, a personality is, a child is, a father is, a mother is, a family is. God, who saw the mess that had already brought devastation to His creation and to human beings, spoke strongly and gave drastic punishments to show the absolute necessity of living in accordance with the truth about who man is as well as the truth about who He is, the Maker and Creator of all.

Before we go on further concerning the law surrounding the Sabbath in the Old Testament, do read that this same God who made it possible for us to call Him Father spoke strongly to disobedient people doing evil things, urging them to come back to Him and be forgiven.

> "Son of man, say to the house of Israel, 'This is what you are saying: "Our offenses and sins weigh us down, and we are wasting away because of them. How then can we live?"' Say to them, 'As surely as I live, declares the Sovereign Lord, I take no pleasure in the death of the wicked, but rather that they turn from their ways and live. Turn! Turn from your evil ways! Why will you die, O house of Israel!' " (Ezekiel 33:10, 11)

The living, holy, everlasting Creator, who gave the Ten Commandments to enable people to know how to live in relationship with Him and with each other, is a compassionate God. He opened the way to come back to Him, to recognize sin as sin and to turn away from it and back to Him. The balance of His love and compassion and His perfect holiness and wisdom is something that we in our own lack of balance, our own imperfections, our own spoiledness, cannot comprehend, except partially. However, as we hear of the warnings given, we should think about the seriousness of the breaking of God's commandments. We must try to recognize that many other people's lives and children's lives, not only in our time, but for all eternity, are affected when people turn away from the law of God. God gave the commandments because He has perfect knowledge of their necessity for human beings to live in a proper relationship with Him, with each other, and with themselves, inside their own heads and hearts.

In Exodus 31:12-18, we are allowed to stand on Mount Sinai with Moses and hear what God has to say concerning the Sabbaths.

> Then the Lord said to Moses, "Say to the Israelites, 'You must observe my Sabbaths. This will be a sign between me and you for the generations to come, so you may know I am the Lord, who makes you holy. Observe the Sabbath, because it is holy to you. Anyone who desecrates it must be put to death; whoever does any work on that day must be cut off from his people. For six days work is to be done, but the seventh day is a Sabbath of rest, holy to the Lord. Whoever does any work on the Sabbath day must be put to death. The Israelites are to observe the Sabbath, celebrating it for generations to come as a lasting covenant. It will be a sign between me and the Israelites forever, for in six days the Lord made the heavens and the earth, and on the seventh day he abstained from work and rested.' "
>
> When the Lord finished speaking to Moses on Mount Sinai, he gave him the two tablets of the Testimony, the tablets of stone inscribed by the finger of God.

Human beings have a basic reaction against rules, commandments, laws. They feel they are not serious, that anyone can choose what he or she will term as right or wrong—even if they do not have a base to choose from. The large community of Israelites had not only been living among people who worshiped false gods, and who based their lives on a false base, but they themselves had just proved how fickle and shallow their own loyalty, trust, belief, and love for the true God was, in their constant grumbling, in their turning to worship an idol, and in their misuse of His name. Now they are being told both that the Sabbath is not a gift to be taken or not, according to whim, and also that it is to be a day that will be a very lasting, serious, solemn *sign* that they belong to God, are His people, and are different from the people of surrounding nations who do not worship Him or acknowledge His existence. This Sabbath day is to be a sign to anyone watching—other people, angels, demons, anyone in the universe—that there is a covenant, an agreement, a relationship between God and His own people.

One seventh of time, one twenty-four-hour period out of seven times twenty-four hours, one day out of seven, is to be a day to look back at the amazing reality of God's having worked to create the earth in six days, and then having rested the seventh. It does not matter here whether God's creation was six twenty-four-hour days (whatever your understanding of the word "day" is in relation to creation); the thing that matters is that God has said that He made the earth in six days. The seventh day, or one seventh of the same length of time, He, the Creator, who we are told never is tired or weary, rested from creating all that He created.

What does that mean?

It means a tremendously important thing. Just because we cannot dissect and analyze all that God means when He tells us He rested, or when He tells us He has hallowed this day and blessed it to be a special day, does not mean we are to toss it out as a concept we can't get to the bottom of.

The Creator is speaking to all human beings; He has made it the fourth commandment in the first four relating to our duties to God. We are to respect this day; He has commanded us to respect it.

Surely that means how much time we set aside to think about Him and His mighty works, how much time we spend reading, discussing, and considering His Word. It means trying to work out in our own piece of history, our own lifetime, our own spot of the earth, in the midst of our own circumstances—whether a farm or a concentration camp—some practical way of carrying out the fourth commandment. This is not to be shoved out because it is uncomfortable to contemplate. Of course God can give us strength in our weakness in the midst of the rush of work and a deluge of business. Of course He is always the same and never sleeps or becomes weary. Yet our Heavenly Father has made it emphatically definite that this proportion of time set aside to be different in some practical way is to be a sign, an outward sign of an inward reality, that we are His people.

Was this only in the Old Testament? Did Christ do away with it? Christ made clear that the Pharisees and others like them had for centuries been making up a list of legalistic, man-made additions which became a dangerous religious practice. What is the constant danger? The danger is always the same—that people will make up laws to add to what the Bible has said, and then in keeping those lists, forget the inward turning away from the God they claim to be worshiping. In Matthew 23:25-27 Jesus speaks very strongly to any who felt pious because they kept a list of details when their basic attitude toward God and their preparation to recognize the Messiah was all wrong. They were so proud of their religiosity they were not even conscious of their sin.

"Woe to you, teachers of the law and Pharisees, you hypocrites! You clean the outside of the cup and dish, but inside they are full of greed and self-indulgence. Blind Pharisees! First clean the inside of the cup and dish, and then the outside also will be clean.

"Woe to you, teachers of the law and Pharisees, you hypocrites! You are like whitewashed tombs, which look beautiful on the outside but on the inside are full of dead men's bones and everything unclean. In the same way, on the outside you appear to people as righteous but on the inside you are full of hypocrisy and wickedness."

Jesus shows very clearly the ugliness that comes from making an outward show of piousness when the reality of carrying out what God teaches through the ages is being made into an empty, hollow farce. This He emphasized in connection with the Sabbath observance.

Come to Mark 2:22—3:6.

One Sabbath Jesus was going through the grainfields, and as his disciples walked along, they began to pick some heads of grain. The Pharisees said to him, "Look, why are they doing what is unlawful on the Sabbath?"

He answered, "Have you never read what David did when he and his companions were hungry and in need? In the days of Abiathar the high priest, he entered the house of God and ate the consecrated bread, which is lawful only for priests to eat. And he also gave some to his companions." Then he said to them, "The Sabbath was made for man, not man for the Sabbath. So the Son of Man is Lord even of the Sabbath."

Another time he went into the synagogue, and a man with a shriveled hand was there. Some of them were looking for a reason to accuse Jesus, so they watched him closely to see if he would heal him on the Sabbath. Jesus said to the man with the shriveled hand, "Stand up in front of everyone." Then Jesus asked them, "Which is lawful on the Sabbath: to do good or to do evil, to save life or to kill?" But they remained silent!

He looked around them in anger and, deeply distressed at their stubborn hearts, said to the man, "Stretch out your hand." He stretched it out, and his hand was completely restored. Then the Pharisees went out and began to plot with the Herodians how they might kill Jesus.

In Luke, Jesus demonstrates once again the fuller meaning of keeping the law of God in relation to the Sabbath. After all, we are told that Jesus kept all the law perfectly and did not sin in one tiny detail. Jesus the Christ, the Messiah, the Lamb of God, lived a perfect life for us, and died a perfect death for us. He is our example. He is demonstrating what the difference is between having the "outside of the cup clean, and the inside filthy" and a true cleanliness of the whole person, the kind of obedience that pleases God.

It was on another Sabbath when Jesus was teaching in one of the synagogues when a crippled woman came to Jesus, bent over and unable to straighten up. She had been like this for eighteen years. Jesus had compassion on her and set her free from this infirmity.

Indignant because Jesus had healed on the Sabbath, the synagogue ruler said to the people, "There are six days for work. So come and be healed on those days, not on the Sabbath." The Lord answered him, "You hypocrites! Doesn't each of you on the Sabbath untie his ox or donkey from the stall and lead it out to give it water? Then should not this woman, a daughter of Abraham, whom Satan has kept bound for eighteen long years, be set free on the Sabbath day from what bound her?" When he said this, all his opponents were humiliated, but the people were delighted with all the wonderful things he was doing. (Luke 13:14-17)

Along with these incidents, we need also to remember the Sabbath-day healing told about in John. Jesus was walking along by the pool near the Sheep Gate in Jerusalem when he saw a paralyzed man who had been an invalid for thirty-eight years lying beside the pool.

> Then Jesus said to him, "Get up! Pick up your mat and walk." At once the man was cured; he picked up his mat and walked. The day on which this took place was a Sabbath, and so the Jews said to the man who had been healed, "It is the Sabbath; the law forbids you to carry your mat." But he replied, "The man who made me well said to me, 'Pick up your mat and walk.' " So they asked him, "Who is this fellow who told you to pick it up and walk?" (John 5:8-12)

Then go on to John 5:16-18.

> So, because Jesus was doing these things on the Sabbath, the Jews persecuted him. Jesus said to them, "My Father is always at his work to this very day, and I, too, am working." For this reason the Jews tried all the harder to kill him; not only was he breaking the Sabbath, but he was even calling God his own Father, making himself equal with God.

Jesus goes on to say many things about Himself, explaining that God the Father has entrusted all judgment to Him so that all people will honor the Son just as they honor the Father.

In the context of the Sabbath day, and what the law means in our lives, it is very interesting that Jesus opens up new and very deep understanding about how judgment is to be made. He who is the Judge says that the Sabbath was made for man, that it is to be a day which is helpful to people in meeting real needs. He who is Judge said that helping sick people, doing practical things for disabled people, people in need, is very in keeping with the Sabbath's meaning. He who will be Judge when everyone will appear before Him, either in the believer's judgment, or in the judgment of unbelievers, has Himself shown that when the disciples were hungry it was a good thing for them to satisfy that physical hunger by picking some food from a harvest, ready and ripe to be picked, enough to satisfy that hunger. He showed immediate compassion to the people who needed His help, and He helped them because they needed it, because it was right in God's eyes. He did not care what impression it made on the religious leaders or the pious religious people. He did not try to impress them so that they would listen to Him more.

How many of us do things to make an impression on some other human beings rather than caring to do what is right in the eyes of God, in the eyes of our Savior and Lord, the One who will be our Judge. What really matters is finding out by daily searching His Word what He would have us do. To care about His law enough to search His Word and talk to Him about it in prayer, as well as to talk to each other about it in the family, to change what we are doing if we discover we have been making a mistake, to have courage to confess we have been charging ahead in sin and need to stop and find out where we went off the track—that is what is needed in the last years of the twentieth century, as much as at the time when Jesus was walking on the earth and pointing out to religious people that they were *way* off the track!

You and I need to be serious about the possibility of Jesus saying to us, "Woe to you, you hypocrites." We are not free from the danger of getting entangled with outward things while our inward realities are not what they should be.

Why were the Pharisees so far off the track? What had been given in their Scriptures that they had paid no attention to? What are we apt to be neglecting today?

Come back to Isaiah 58 first.

> "If you keep your feet from breaking the Sabbath
>   and from doing as you please on my holy day,
> if you call the Sabbath a delight
>   and the Lord's holy day honorable,
> and if you honor it by not going your own way
>   and not doing as you please or speaking idle words,
> then you will find your joy in the Lord,
>   and I will cause you to ride on the heights of the land
> and to feast on the inheritance of your father Jacob."
> The mouth of the Lord has spoken.
>
> (vv. 13, 14)

This day which is to be different is meant to be a delight, a day when we discover that joy is found in the Lord. There are promises connected with seriously trying to do what honors the Lord and not engaging in a selfish, egotistical search for one's own pleasure. "Honor it . . . by not doing as you please" seems to speak of this.

But if you will look back over this chapter, you will find that it begins with the Israelites asking God why He hasn't noticed their fasting and humbling themselves. And God tells them it is because they have been doing as they pleased on the days of fasting, which seems to be the exploiting of their workers. God says strongly to them that He is not interested in fasting and prayer as pious religious exercises; He does not choose to be sought after that way. We will go into this passage again in another commandment, but for the moment it is important that preceding the admonition about not breaking the Sabbath day comes this outline of things that matter to Him—things such as, "loosing the chains of injustice, untying the cords of the yoke, to set the oppressed free"; things like "sharing food with the hungry, providing the poor wanderer with shelter, clothing the naked, and not turning away from our own flesh and blood." These are practical things that God cares about. To turn away from being human to other human beings and to be totally selfish in religious exercises, even in sackcloth and ashes with fasting and prayer, is not what God is pleased with.

This ties in very specifically with what Jesus demonstrated on the Sabbath day as the way to please God. He cared for people who had a variety of needs. Surely part of the observance of the one different day in the week, in addition to it being a day of rest from our ordinary six days of work, is that we are to be ready to care for the hungry, sick, broken, and needy people who especially need our care. They need to be people living near us, if we are to do something practically and personally. We cannot say, "If I had lived then," or "If I could be in such and such a location . . ." "then I would do thus and so."

In 1862 Christopher Wordsworth wrote a hymn around this passage in Isaiah 58:13, which we have just quoted.

> O day of rest and gladness,
>   O day of joy and light,
> O balm of care and sadness,
>   Most beautiful, most bright;
> On thee the high and lowly,
>   Through ages joined in tune.
> Sing Holy, Holy, Holy,
>   To the great God Triune.

We usually sing it to a tune written by Lowell Mason in 1839 in Germany, then later arranged. How staggering to think of well over a hundred years of tiny children who have become old people, and more tiny children holding parents' hands as they stand on chairs or church pews to sing these words. What has it meant to people? To many of them it has meant something very real—a day to join with those they see in their own locality, with all the unseen people throughout all the time zones of the world, and with all the people now in heaven who sang it on earth, worshiping and singing with a measure of love and appreciation to God, the Creator, who commanded that one day in seven be different. It is a hymn about this different day as one man understood it.

What day of the week is the one day now? There are some who keep Saturday as a day of worship, the seventh day of the week, the Sabbath of the Old Testament. There are many, many other people who are certain that as the Jewish passover led up to the moment of Christ the Messiah, the Lamb of God's death, so the Lord Jesus Himself introduced the Lord's Supper now to look back to His death as the Lamb. The day of the resurrection of the Lamb, the resurrection of the body of the Lord Jesus Christ, was to be the new day to set aside each week as the day of worship.

You remember that it was the first day of the week that Jesus rose from the dead.

> On the evening of that first day of the week, when the disciples were together, with the doors locked for fear of the Jews, Jesus came and stood among them and said, "Peace be with you!" After He said this, he showed them his hands and side. The disciples were overjoyed when they saw the Lord. Again Jesus said, "Peace be with you! As the Father has sent me, I am sending you." (John 20:19-21)

Then in the book of Acts, it seems to me to be clear that the first day of the week was the day for the gathering together of the Christians in the homes of various ones. In Acts 20:7-12, the scene is Troas.

> On the first day of the week we came together to break bread. Paul spoke to the people and, because he intended to leave the next day, kept on talking until midnight. There were many lamps in the upstairs room where we were meeting. Seated in a window was a young man

named Eutychus, who was sinking into a deep sleep as Paul talked on and on. When he was sound asleep, he fell to the ground from the third story and was picked up dead. Paul went down, threw himself on the young man and put his arms around him. "Don't be alarmed," he said. "He's alive!" Then he went upstairs again and broke bread and ate. After talking until daylight, he left. The people took the young man home alive and were greatly comforted.

There are several things that should be a help to us in thinking about how to use our Sundays. This passage makes it known that the Christians gathered together to "break bread," to have communion together. It also shows us that Paul spoke for hours and hours. He was leaving the next day, so it was an opportunity they wouldn't have again. This was no short service, but a time of teaching and coming to further understanding. We may have a good idea about what Paul taught as we read his epistles or his sermon on Mars Hill. It would be deep and full and practical. Does this mean we should be up all night long every Sunday? I think not! But in addition to the example of Jesus showing us we are to care for the needs of people, and in addition to the passage we have considered from Isaiah, there is this which lets us know we are expected to continue to have time with other Christians breaking bread and pursuing the knowledge and understanding which would lead to *doing* the Word of God in a more realistic way during the week.

Be very careful, then, how you live—not as unwise, but as wise, making the most of every opportunity, because the days are evil. Therefore do not be foolish, but understand what the Lord's will is. Do not get drunk on wine, which leads to debauchery. Instead, be filled with the Spirit. Speak to one another with psalms, hymns and spiritual songs. Sing and make music in your heart to the Lord, always giving thanks to God the Father for everything, in the name of our Lord Jesus Christ. (Ephesians 5:15-20)

The "day of rest and gladness" is to continue; it is not to be thrown away because we do not live in Old Testament times. It is to be a day of rest, of difference, of helping other people whether by going to them, or opening some sort of hospitality. It is to be a day of studying the Word of God to understand better what His will is, a day of making music, whether silently in our hearts, or audibly with instruments and voices. Alone with the family, in small or larger groups—there is no set of rules for exactly how to schedule these twenty-four hours. The person to please is the Lord Himself.

What else?

> Now about the collection for God's people: Do what I told the Galatian churches to do. On the first day of every week, each one of you should set aside a sum of money in keeping with his income, saving it up, so that when I come no collections will have to be made. Then, when I arrive, I will give letters of introduction to the men you approve and send them with your gift to Jerusalem. If it seems advisable for me to go also, they will accompany me. (1 Corinthians 16:1-4)

Giving a portion of one's material goods to the Lord, as well as giving one day of the week to both rest and honor Him, was part of God's teaching through Moses, as well as through Paul to the Galatians and Corinthians. It was a part of the reality of being a person who acknowledged and bowed before God in true communication and a true relationship. It is very important to note that the amount was to be "in keeping with his income," indicating that the early church Christians had differing incomes week after week. They were to share with those who had need, but they had something to share, and they had various amounts to share. Talents and gifts differ. It is a proportion that is to be given to the Lord, whether it is the "cup of cold water" and the "when I was sick ye cared for me" way of giving to Him, or a proportion of income.

The first day of the week, when there was time and a regularity of checking up on oneself in a variety of areas, was meant to be the time to go over the accounts sufficiently to know what a proper "portion" would be.

In the Old Testament it was a tithe that was to be given to the Lord, and one cannot imagine that God meant to have us give less after Christ had come and died and made it possible for us to be His children, "some from every tribe and nation," as we are now.

Surely our one day in seven should be a day when we consider as a family, or as individuals, whether we have been carrying out practically what the Lord would have us do in His other commandments. This should be a day when, as we walk in the woods, a park, a country lane, a beach, a city sidewalk (where perhaps we can see a tree), in addition to other creative thoughts we may have, or ideas as to how to live more honestly in the light of God's Word, we spend some time talking to each other, or thinking and praying, about how we can fulfill the admonitions in Romans 12:9-16 (read the whole chapter):

> Love must be sincere. Hate what is evil; cling to what is good. Be devoted to one another in brotherly love. Honor one another above yourselves. Never be lacking in zeal, but keep your spiritual fervor, serving the Lord. Be joyful in hope, patient in affliction, faithful in prayer. Share with God's people who are in need. Practice hospitality. Bless those who persecute you; bless and do not curse. Rejoice with those who rejoice; mourn with those who mourn. Live in harmony with one another. Do not be proud, but be willing to associate with people of low position. Do not be conceited.

Sunday is a day for being alone with family, at least some of the time, if at all possible. But to "practice hospitality" there needs to be food prepared to share, and a door open to someone who will walk in and spoil the aloneness! Sunday is a day to review the week and to find out how much hospitality has been practiced, and with whom anything has been shared, whether a meal, or a pair of shoes, or money to pay for medicine, or a vacation given to a weary mother or sick worker. There are practical checkups to take place.

What has this to do with simply going to church and sighing with relief that our duty to God is over with? Not much. We are not to judge each other, but we do need to judge—each one himself, or herself—how well we have provided for the strong place the fourth commandment is to have in our practical lives.

"But," you may say, "you haven't spelled out the details of what we can do on Sunday in the twentieth century to keep the commandment as God means us to do today." I believe this is what the Lord gave us the Old and New Testament for—that with the help of the Holy Spirit, we might read and pray and ask for help in the practical things that apply to our own situation in Hong Kong, in Seoul, in Nigeria, in San Francisco, in Caracas, in the Swiss Alps, in Boston, in Vancouver, in Paris, in Hawaii, in Alaska, in South Africa, in South America, in the deserts, in the jungles, in prison, in hospitals, in nursing homes, in homes of atheistic parents, in institutions where few choices are open. There are no set rules which can be followed by each person because of our very diverse situations. Thank God that He "looks upon the hearts." He knows who truly loves Him; He knows who has a desire both to be and do that which would be pleasing to Him.

It is a fearful thing to be doing the outward things as correctly as the Pharisees were doing them and to be filthy inside where the Lord is judging our sincerity so that His word to us is, "you hypocrite!" Our great concern should be to be doing before Him—in opposition to whatever Satan would be trying to hinder us from doing—that which demonstrates our inward reality. Outward conformity means nothing to God.

We also are called to help little children in our families, neighborhoods, churches, or schools, to have some idea of the imagination and creativity that can result in a really looked-forward-to "Sabbath of rest to the Lord," which is a different kind of day, but a warm joyous one.

It is six forty-five on a Saturday night as I write this chapter's ending. The bells of all the churches in Switzerland have begun to ring. Deep-throated bells, higher bells with a variety of notes, heavy bells with slow, heavy dongs, lighter, faster bells trying to do two notes to others' one, ringing out over the mountains, over the lakes, over the cities, over the villages, for fifteen full minutes.

Who listens to them today, in the last period of the twentieth century? What thoughts come into the minds of those who do listen? Many years ago when Christianity predominated, they were the call to prepare for Sunday, to get the children bathed and clothing ready for the morning, to have the bread and pies and cakes prepared for the Sunday meal, to have the house tidied and brushed up for a day of "rest and gladness," a day without the usual work in fields, factories, gardens, a day when floor scrubbings and window washing would be put aside. The bells say so many things, with so many different ears hearing them and such a variety of responses.

We often wish we could go back to what seemed like a simpler day and obey the admonition of the bells quietly, ready to go to church without any rush, to walk, quietly gathering flowers in the afternoon in season, or to bundle up against the cold and ski or snowshoe, to sit by the fire eating an apple and drinking hot "ovo" while *Pilgrim's Progress* is being read, to get out the special Sunday toys to be played with only on the rug by the fireside, to write a letter and draw pictures for grandmother, or Aunt Prisca or Aunt Sue or Debby or Genie, excitedly realizing that communication could reach them this way as well as to have the wonder of singing together as a family, and praying for the ones who have left to be at school or married or working in a distant country.

Saturday night bells and a nostalgia for a quieter century! But can't we with determination to put first things first, and with God's help, prepare for a day that will be within the possibility of our circumstances and geographical location, a different day that will be very real as a reminder of what God has given in the past and of that fabulous rest He is preparing for in the future? There is a day coming that will indeed be our rest, and a time of rest and restoration for all nature.

Right now, however, we need to prepare for the Lord's Day each week in a sincere and very real way, so that we and our children may know something of the keeping of the fourth commandment now, for "rest and gladness" as well as worship, for God's glory as well as man's good.

5: THE FIFTH COMMANDMENT

Swarms of refugees stumble, drag their feet, or trudge briskly out of an increasing number of homelands, across marshes and fields, through woods or jungles, frightened, confused, broken in body and mind. Crowds of refugees bob in boats, or swim endless stretches of dangerous waters, in a vast number of seas or rivers, leaving an uncountable number of former homes that had been in the family for years. Displaced persons! What a tragedy of the twentieth century! There have been more displaced persons in recent years than in all of the combined centuries before. Displaced from familiar lands, from crops that grew year after year in the same gardens or fields. Displaced from familiar continuity of family groupings with three generations living on the same spot.

These pictures stir emotions. Our eyes sting with sudden tears at the thought of human beings who can never know anything of real continuity again—aliens in an alien surrounding, facing a bleak childhood, a bleak middle age, an even bleaker old age.

In countries where people can stay in safety and have no need to run from their own familiar towns and villages, where the year is marked by the country fair, the winter concert series or the autumn circus, where continuity is tangible—there is a new flood of "displaced persons" torn away from homes and possessions and other members of their families by the strange and twisted teaching that they must, at all costs, fight for their "rights." Putting personal rights in first place, before any other person, ends up in destroying all the continuity that God made human beings to be able to have. Who am I? cries the displaced person. What will fulfill me? Broken families, splintered into scattered bits, make displaced persons out of people who live in lands which are not yet invaded by an alien enemy. A broken family scatters the priceless collection of things handed down from generation to generation. Thus, the comfortable feeling of snuggling down under grandmother's quilt becomes a forgotten part of life, never to be experienced by many children born at the end of the twentieth century. Divorced parents, called single parents, try to give their own displaced children something of a feeling of continuity even as they struggle over the displaced feeling inside themselves.

Families were meant to be a continuity with generation following generation—not a confused mixture of splinters as broken as the scattered families of refugees. How many real refugees there are in the world, made up of frustrated people trying to find out who they are, if you count all the broken relationships in thrice, or twice, or once divorced couples and their children! They cling to bits of wreckage seeking some solid ground to start life on the other side of the divorce—as stormy a body of water to cross as any gale-blown gulf or sea or ocean.

Displaced people. Refugees. People breaking God's pattern for living. People for whom humanness has been lost along the way.

Now there is a new idea of how to break up families and relationships, being taught as a new "freedom," a new certainty of having one's "rights." I quote from the *International Herald Tribune* of August 12, 1980, from an article by Jonathan Kandell concerning the new "social experimentation" in Sweden. In speaking of the new bill passed in parliament that parents cannot spank their children (yes, it is illegal to spank your child in Sweden), he says:

One mother recently recounted that she was about to spank her six-year-old boy when he informed her that she would be violating the law. "I asked him how he knew that, and he told me that his teacher had explained to his class about the new legislation," she said. "What really bothered me was that the teacher also asked the kids who were spanked to raise their hands and talk about it." More typical reactions to the new statute seem to range from amusement to disinterest. But this has not deterred a government committee from recently proposing a law that would give children the right to divorce their parents.

What a new freedom to march for! Children to be given freedom to divorce their parents! Young human beings cut off from any ties, free to follow their own whims and desires. Free? What lies are being believed. This freedom is on the same level as the freedom to divorce the Garden of Eden, to divorce life itself, to be free from walking and talking with God, walking and talking with close understanding of other human beings, and finally free from under- standing oneself. "Who am I?" "I don't understand myself at all." "I don't want to live with me." Displaced people are really those who either know nothing of the law of God which unfolds to us *who* human beings are as made in His image, or who have divorced themselves from reading, meditating upon, speaking about, or attempting in any tiny measure to follow His law. In a very real sense those English Punks I spoke about in an earlier chapter had only dressed themselves to look outwardly like many people look inwardly, people who have revolted against being human and who are trying to be something God did not make them to be.

What is the fifth commandment?

This is the first commandment of the second portion of the Ten Commandments. The first portion dealt with our relationship with God; these next six deal with our relationship with other human beings. This one is first in that second series.

"Honor your father and mother, so that you may live long in the land the Lord your God is giving you" (Exodus 20:12).

Read it again as it was written in Leviticus 19:3, where various laws are being given. "Each of you must respect his mother and father, and you must observe my Sabbaths. I am the Lord your God."

Both mother and father are spoken of with a togetherness that indicates the need to respect or honor both. It also indicates they are together, in a constant relationship with each other as well as with the children who are being told that they should continue that respect. The child is not meant to make a choice between the two, but to carry out that respect and honor in some form that is within the realm of possibility at various times of life's history.

The promise to the Israelites as they began to live in the land that God had given to them was that the careful continuity of possessing, farming, caring for, and living on a piece of land would be a family heritage for generations. Being truly human involves family relationships with, first of all, the child-parent relationship, and then the continuity of a "homestead," a place, a piece of terrain, a piece of land, an acre, a garden and house, a tent and a hillside, a boat and a bit of water, a cave in a rock and some land to plant potatoes. By binding together the law with a promise, God showed what He meant by the peaceful life He wanted for His children, if they would follow His law and live by His Word.

First Kings 4:25 gives us a descriptive sentence of such a period of time: "And Judah and Israel dwelt safely, every man under his vine and under his fig tree, from Dan even to Beer-sheba, all the days of Solomon" (KJV).

Let's review again what the parents were to be teaching the children. These children, who were to respect and honor their parents, were to hear day after day things which would make them truly understand the flow of human relationships, the proper relationship with God, and life on the land which God would provide. The fifth commandment was to be taught daily, not as a harsh command—"You'd better respect me, you brat"—but in the context of what all of them had experienced as families in the past as God had brought them out of slavery to a place where living together was a possibility.

Go back to Deuteronomy again.

Hear, O Israel: The Lord our God, the Lord is one. Love the Lord your God with all your heart and with all your soul and with all your strength. These commandments that I give you today are to be upon your hearts. Impress them on your children. Talk about them when you sit at home and when you walk along the road, when you lie down and when you get up. . . . When the Lord your God brings you into the land he swore to your fathers, to Abraham, Isaac and Jacob, to give you—a land with large, flourishing cities you did not build, houses filled with good things you did not provide, wells you did not dig, and vineyards and olive groves you did not plant—then when you eat and are satisfied, be careful that you do not forget the Lord, who brought you out of Egypt, out of the land of slavery. (Deuteronomy 6:4-7, 10-12)

God is talking about communication here, making the family history known to children, as each family would have stories to tell of the details of their experience in the midst of all that had happened and all that God had done for them. If all this had been carried out, love and respect would have followed naturally in many cases.

The command to respect and honor mother and father is very carefully tied in with both mother and father respecting the law of God, not forgetting to teach their children, and encouraging them by answering their questions. God meant families to have true humanness in a relationship of communication.

In Proverbs 1:8 the parents being described are parents who have truly worthwhile teaching to give, but who obviously are able to communicate in a way that would give understanding.

> Listen, my son, to your father's instruction
> and do not forsake your mother's teaching.
> They will be a garland to grace your head
> and a chain to adorn your neck.

Proverbs 4:1-5 gives another beautiful picture of a father and mother who are pointing their child to truth and understanding. Since the previous chapter has made clear that one's own understanding is not sufficient, it is certain that it is the Lord being pointed to.

> Listen, my sons, to a father's instruction;
> pay attention and gain understanding.
> I give you sound learning,
> so do not forsake my teaching.
> When I was a boy in my father's house,
> still tender, and an only child of my mother,
> he taught me and said,
> "Lay hold of my words with all your heart;
> keep my commands and you will live.
> Get wisdom, get understanding;
> do not forget my words or swerve from them."

All fathers and mothers, however, did *not* stay true to the Lord, obey His commandments, teach their children properly, or give good counsel, good advice. When fathers and mothers turned away from God and turned to idols, it always affected their children.

This is made clear to us in both Old and New Testaments. The failure to give either true teaching or a right example to children makes the father and mother a detriment to the next generation. Sadly, this breaks or rips up the pattern that is meant to be handed down and protected.

Remember in 2 Chronicles 22:2, 3, as the very bad King Ahaziah came to reign, his mother is mentioned as having been a terrible hindrance to him in doing right.

> Ahaziah was twenty-two years old when he became king, and he reigned in Jerusalem one year. His mother's name was Athaliah, a granddaughter of Omri. He too walked in the ways of the house of Ahab, for his mother encouraged him in doing wrong. He did evil in the eyes of the Lord, as the house of Ahab had done, for after his father's death they became his advisers, to his undoing.

And in Jeremiah 2:5-8 the Lord points out that fathers strayed far from following Him, and of course this means they did not teach their children the right things at all, nor tell them the law of God.

> This is what the Lord says:
> "What fault did your fathers find in me,
>   that they strayed so far from me?
> They followed worthless idols
>   and became worthless themselves.
> They did not ask, 'Where is the Lord,
>   who brought us up out of Egypt
> and who led us through the barren wilderness,
>   through a land of deserts and rifts,
> a land of drought and darkness,
>   a land where no one travels and no one lives?'
> I brought you into a fertile land
>   to eat its fruit and rich produce.
> But you came and defiled my land
>   and made my inheritance detestable.
> The priests did not ask,
>   'Where is the Lord?'
> Those who deal with the law did not know me;
>   the leaders rebelled against me.
> The prophets prophesied by Baal,
>   following worthless idols.

The only possible way the children of such mothers and fathers as described here could follow the Lord would be to turn away from the idols and false teaching of their mothers and fathers and turn to the Lord.

God speaks very strongly to a generation of children to turn away from the idols of their fathers and to turn to Him, their Sovereign Lord. Ezekiel 20:30 says, "Therefore say to the house of Israel: 'This is what the Sovereign Lord says: Will you defile yourselves the way your fathers did and lust after their vile images?' "

To honor one's father and mother, to respect them and care for them, does not include following the false teaching or idol worship of a mother and father who have turned away from God. God leaves no doubt of this in His Word.

However, if one's parents are Buddhists, or materialistic atheists, there are still ways of treating them humanly, keeping in communication, at least to the level of talking about food, clothing, shelter, the world news, art, or music in some measure to them. If one's parents are unbelievers, a believing child should write letters, remember to send surprises for birthdays, and give as imaginative and loving care as is within the means of the child. Private help, given without the parents realizing it, must also be given. This is constant intercession, faithful prayer for their eyes of understanding to be open. To take a stand against the wrong teaching or even evil practices still means one's parents should be treated as human beings. The door must be left open.

In considering the fifth commandment, we need to check up on the ways we could practically show respect and honor, in the biblical definition of love. There needs to be a sharp distinction between turning away from the false gods and even wicked advice of parents, and the turning away from the parents themselves. Practical ways of long-suffering and kindness can be thought about and then carried out. Physical needs should be cared for.

We are forcibly brought up short time after time when we read 1 Timothy 5:8—"If anyone does not provide for his relatives, and especially for his immediate family, he has denied the faith and is worse than an unbeliever."

This needs to be read and reread, and we need to ask ourselves over and over again what it means to care for the needs of our own families, insofar as we are able to financially. However, there are practical things to be done. How often do we cook special food, take baskets of fruit, pick flowers and arrange them, knit sweaters or shawls, make clothing, provide vacations, send books or chocolates, send grapefruit or apples in season, provide special labor-saving devices as people become disabled or grow older? How much do we think about how we can provide for our family or relatives? We are worse than unbelievers if we do not, so we are told!

But the commandment to honor and respect our father and mother surely includes everything we should do for relatives and more. The commandment points up care of aged parents, and the provision of everything we are able to do for them. It does not mean we have to spend all our money and all our energy so that children and husband or wife and other relatives are robbed of attention. It does not mean that single sons or daughters caring for parents are to have no life of their own. But it does mean a checkup to see whether we have rationalized away every need and every kind of meaning that command has for us in the end of the twentieth century!

Euthanasia is a very dangerous rationalization which entices twentieth-century people to consider how very dignified it would be to choose to die at exactly the opportune moment. There are two books out in England now which go into detail on how to commit suicide and thus avoid living when it is no longer attractive. That manual as to how to commit suicide can be accepted as easily as the idea of children divorcing parents! If a child can choose to divorce his or her parents when the child is still a teenager, imagine the mentality that would carry into a later period of life and would turn that idea of divorce of a parent into putting pressure on that parent "just to swallow this pill and leave us gracefully." The deception of the human heart has been so excruciatingly demonstrated through the years that making such an idea a "topic of conversation" and the "subject of books" brings it within the realm of respectability.

The sweeping acceptance of the idea of euthanasia is, among other things, a terrible temptation to break the fifth commandment in a drastic way. Satan is very clever in his temptations to break God's commandments. Since he is so vigilant in looking for new ways to tempt human beings away from God's commands, he would pounce upon this new way of getting people to break the fifth commandment. If someone would listen to him, Satan could get a person to kill his or her father or mother, or persuade that parent to commit suicide, while deceiving himself or herself that it was being done for "dignity's sake." The warning about the devil given in 1 Peter 5:8 fits in here: "Be self-controlled and alert. Your enemy the devil prowls around like a roaring lion looking for someone to devour. Resist him, standing firm in the faith, because you know that your brothers throughout the world are undergoing the same kind of sufferings."

In Matthew 15, Jesus is talking to a group of Pharisees and teachers of the law concerning the tricky ways they have invented for "keeping the commandments" when in fact they are breaking them. They have made up laws which cancel out the true meaning of the law and enable people to be considered as keeping God's law while they are actually breaking it. The fifth commandment was the illustration Jesus used.

> Then some of the Pharisees and teachers of the law came to Jesus from Jerusalem and asked, "Why do your disciples break the tradition of the elders? They don't wash their hands before they eat!"
>
> Jesus replied, "And why do you break the command of God for the sake of your tradition? For God said, 'Honor your father and mother' and 'Anyone who curses his father or mother must be put to death.' But you say that if a man says to his father or mother, 'Whatever help you might otherwise have received from me is a gift devoted to God,' he is not to 'honor his father' with it. Thus you nullify the word of God for the sake of your tradition. You hypocrites! Isaiah was right when he prophesied about you:
>
> > 'These people honor me with their lips,
> >   but their hearts are far from me.
> > They worship me in vain;
> >   their teachings are but rules taught by men.' "

Jesus is pointing out that this is not really caring for fathers and mothers. Instead of being sure that their fathers and mothers had the necessities of life and were warmly and humanly provided for, which was what God meant by "respect and honor," the traditions which had been added made a loophole whereby people could piously say that they were keeping the law concerning father and mother without really caring for them. It seems the loophole was a kind of ceremonial giving, whereby a gift would be presented to the temple with some kind of ritualistic words said over it, making it a token gift to the father and mother, while in actual fact the father and mother had received nothing, and were being neglected.

It would be as if you and I gave a gift, in the name of our living parents or other living relatives, to some Christian work, and then felt pious about it, thinking we had then carried out the command to honor father and mother and care for our families and relatives—just when a relative badly needed a bunch of flowers in the hospital, a warm winter coat, a vacation because of depression or exhaustion, help in paying the rent, a turkey for thanksgiving, or some other practical help. The word is strongly given to us in 1 Timothy 5:8 in the very context of Jesus talking to the Pharisees here in Matthew: "If anyone does not provide for his relatives, and especially for his immediate family, he has denied the faith and is worse than an unbeliever."

Just as the Pharisees added traditions that gave people the feeling that they were keeping the law while breaking God's serious and basic commands, so today all sorts of religious additions are made. These make people feel that it pleases God more to give gifts to "spiritual" projects than to provide the material, psychological, emotional, intellectual, day-by-day needs of their families. We should think about, pray about, and consider the importance of this balance because the first commandment God gave concerning our relationship to our fellow human beings was the command to care for the needs of our parents and families.

It is not that our responsibility for any wider circle of needy people is blotted out, but there is a strong basic command which we must deal with in honest sincerity, asking for God's wisdom to translate it into action day by day and through the years.

As Paul writes to the congregation of Christians in Ephesus whom he calls "the faithful in Christ Jesus," he tells them that he thanks God for their faith and for their "love for all the saints." Paul therefore considers this group of people a loving group of sincere believers. His admonitions to them are also to all who have lived since and are as definite to us now as to the Ephesians then. The amazing freshness of God's Word should be a marvel to us and fill us with excitement day by day. We *do* have something from God that answers the questions Who am I? and What will fulfill me?

In Ephesians 6:1-4 Paul goes back and quotes the fifth commandment, underlining it again as meant for now, along with the promise that God gave with it.

> Children, obey your parents in the Lord, for this is right. "Honor your father and mother"—which is the first commandment with a promise—"that it may go well with you and that you may enjoy long life on the earth." Fathers, do not exasperate your children; instead, bring them up in the training and instruction of the Lord.

The first thing to notice is that the commandment, the law, has not been tossed out from our consideration now. The law has not been deleted because we are now under grace. Of course we are certain of our salvation because our sins really have been forgiven on the basis of Christ's having been the Lamb of God who died as our substitute. Of course, we cannot keep the law perfectly and we need constant forgiveness. But we are given instruction as Christians now, who sit listening along with the church at Ephesus, shoulder to shoulder, eager to find out how to live in a way that will be in keeping with truth, the truth of who we are, what God made us to be, as well as the truth of God's law.

The second thing to notice is that the children who need to obey their parents are young enough to be included in that word of warning to the fathers a sentence later, that they do not exasperate their children but "bring them up in the training and instruction of the Lord." There is a period of time during which we are being "brought up," and that period of time comes to an end. We speak of children, young people, middle-aged people, and old people. And although the lines are not hard and fast, there is indeed a difference between being brought up and that period of life when being brought up is behind one forever, that stage that ushers in the time of living directly before the Lord, getting instructions from Him, and making one's own mistakes!

Here I am, a sixty-six-year-old grandmother. My father died only four years ago at the age of 101. In a real sense I was his child for all those years, but in time we became adults, brother and sister in the family of the Lord, on the same level. Yet he remained my father whom I needed to respect and honor and care for in practical ways. That, of course, lasts throughout life in a diversity of ways, in balance with what God is unfolding as my work as the years go on.

I cannot say such and such is the age when you can stop using the word "obey" and begin to use "advise" and "discuss." The transition does come, however. Just because we are twenty years older than our children does not mean that if we live a particularly long life the children cannot ever become adults and be directly responsible before God, making choices, asking His help, and preparing to be parents themselves. This is exactly what generations are all about!

It is important right here to go back to Genesis, before the fall, before sin had entered the world, before thorns, thirst, sickness, death, ugliness, violence, devastation had had any place at all. At this time when all creation was perfect and nothing had come in to spoil it, after Adam had been created a grown-up man, an adult, we find a beautiful answer to Who am I? and What will fulfill me? by seeing what would have been perfect fulfillment had nothing come along to spoil things, to make human beings so selfish, egotistical, and greedy. We find that before death had entered to give an expectation of the human relationships having a termination point, to give an ending to the parent-child relationship by the previous generation not being around any longer, that there was in fact a very amazingly sharp distinction made by God of the separateness of the generations, of new families being formed, of the parent-child relationship *not* going on in the same way throughout adult life.

Come to Genesis 2:15-24.

The Lord God took the man and put him in the Garden of Eden to work it and take care of it. And the Lord God commanded the man, "You are free to eat from any tree in the garden; but you must not eat from the tree of the knowledge of good and evil, for when you eat of it you will surely die."

The Lord God said, "It is not good for man to be alone. I will make a helper suitable for him." Now the Lord God had formed out of the ground all the beasts of the field and all the birds of the air. He brought them to the man to see what he would name them; and whatever the man called each living creature, that was its name. So the man gave names to all the livestock, the birds of the air and all the beasts of the field.

But for Adam no suitable helper was found. So the Lord God caused the man to fall into a deep sleep; and while he was sleeping, he took one of the man's ribs and closed up the place with flesh. Then the Lord God made a woman from the rib he had taken out of the man, and he brought her to the man.

The man said,

> "This is now bone of my bones
> and flesh of my flesh;
> she shall be called woman,
> for she was taken out of man."

For this reason a man will leave his father and mother and be united to his wife, and they will become one flesh.

Adam had not had a father and mother; Eve had not had a father and mother. The oneness of their relationship was being given them in a marvelously perfect surrounding and in a way that they could be perfectly sure of who they were and what would fulfill them as they worked in the garden and had communication in the midst of unspoiled love. But before they had a child, before they could experience the passage of time leading to another generation beginning new families, the basic teaching was unfolded, the basic command in human relationships was set forth. The *reason* a person leaves father and mother is to enter into the new relationship of oneness, to start a new generation of the family. The parent-child relationship was never meant to be permanent. Just because a person was born some number of years before his or her child, and was a "parent," that did not mean the child could *never* become mature enough to make decisions and live a separate life. It is striking that God took the trouble to make this clear in giving us evidence that this was His plan for human beings before there was any fall.

You may be asking, "What about single people, people who never marry? Are they to be always under the direction and command of their parents, simply because they have no one to be united to?" We have no way of knowing what the world would have been like if no fall had taken place, if no sin had entered into the world to spoil all that God made. Since the fall there is *nothing* that is perfect—no perfect people, no perfect relationships, no perfect situations, no perfect health, no perfect wisdom. Among other imperfections, there are many people who come to the end of their "being brought up" and are "up," so to speak, and ready to go on as adults making their decisions before the Lord, asking Him directly for help, also ready to make their own mistakes. Whether these people are to be married or to go on alone in careers of a different sort does not affect their being out of the category of being a child who is not yet brought up. The leaving of father and mother is *just* as definite in order to do whatever is before them at that stage of life.

Just as each girl and boy, each woman and man, stands directly before God in coming to a place of believing truth and believing what God has made known in His Word, and bowing before God asking forgiveness and accepting what Christ has done in his or her place, so each person must also have responsibility personally before God for the choices made in life. No mother and father can accept the work of Christ for their children. They can teach the truth, make it exciting, exhibit it in their lives, show forth its reality day by day. But they cannot bow, accept, believe in place of their children. So it is true that each individual is responsible for choices of what to do in life and for seeking directly the help of God. If anyone lacks wisdom, that person is to come individually to God for help. Of course, when parents have made friends early in life with their children, there is valuable discussion and advice that can be helpful. But decisions are the responsibility of each individual; to substitute or transfer the responsibility to parents is like Adam substituting the responsibility of his choice to eat the forbidden fruit to his wife, Eve. We stand alone before God! The Bible makes very clear for any person that there is a primary responsibility, and that is the responsibility to God Himself.

In another book I shall be telling of my husband's struggle in disobeying his parents when they told him he could not study in preparation for the ministry. Later in life there was the same strong cry against his going to Europe, against his staying in Switzerland at the beginning of L'Abri. He came to a certainty that he had to say, "I love you, and I am sorry I have to make you unhappy, but I am convinced that this is what God wants me to do, and I am going to do it." A number of other L'Abri workers, as well as many in God's work throughout history, have had to take the same stand. This is not the place to tell the stories, but in case after case, as in the case with my own husband, the Lord later brought parents to Himself in belief, and also made clear that the work He had called the individual to was indeed His work. There would never have been a L'Abri, nor any of the results which have come forth from it, if that principle of following the Lord in opposition to parents, while still caring lovingly for the parents, had not been carried out.

What does the Bible say about this? As Jesus sends out his disciples to tell of Him, to acknowledge Him before men, to make the gospel known, He speaks of putting the Lord first in the decision of following His call. In Matthew 10:32-42 Jesus is speaking:

"Whoever acknowledges me before men, I will also acknowledge him before my Father in heaven. But whoever disowns me before men, I will disown him before my Father in heaven. Do not suppose that I have come to bring peace to the earth. I did not come to bring peace, but a sword. For I have come to turn

'a man against his father,
a daughter against her mother,
a daughter-in-law against her mother-in-law—
a man's enemies will be the members of his own household.'

"Anyone who loves his father or mother more than me is not worthy of me; anyone who loves his son or daughter more than me is not worthy of me; and anyone who does not take his cross and follow me is not worthy of me. Whoever finds his life will lose it, and whoever loses his life for my sake will find it."

Does this contradict the law which Jesus refers to when talking to the Pharisees about honoring father and mother? Not at all. What is being said is that people are to love the Lord *more* than father and mother, and that in cases where the members of the family do not turn to the Lord but rather turn away from Him, there will be a struggle. It is a battle that has continued through the centuries between those who serve the true and living God, and those who serve idols, false gods, and false prophets. Jesus is stating the fact that loyalty to God comes first, and following Him consists of walking away from the path parents are insisting upon, if it is not the path given in Scripture.

It isn't that the Christian is to be an enemy to the members of his family who do not believe; rather, they will perhaps become enemies to him or her if they continue in their false beliefs.

So very often when people lose their lives, their material possessions, their family's approval, their careers, their rights for the Lord's sake, even in this life it becomes evident that they have found their lives, truly having fulfillment and certainty of the Who am I? Usually when people are losing their lives for following the Lord's path for them, their lives are so extremely busy and full there is no time to stop and count up all the finding that is going on! It is the self-centered insistence on rights and the constant insistence on happiness which ends in losing life. The key is doing things "for my sake," Jesus says.

To finish the story about my husband's going against his parents' commands as he went to college to prepare for the ministry: as we look over the long years that have passed, we know that his obeying the Lord was in the end the means of bringing first his father and later his mother to the Lord. And there is more. The very fact of L'Abri's existence made it more possible to care for my husband's mother the last seven years of her life than would have been the case had we been doing what she had wanted. We have seen this to be true in case after case: leaving father and mother in that sense, coupled with loving care and constant communication with the same father and mother, brings about the finding of life—for the parents, too, as they come to understand and accept and receive eternal life through Jesus Christ.

The centrality of loving the Lord with all our hearts and souls and minds and strength is shown as a basic part of serving Him as Jesus speaks to the rich young ruler. We are told Jesus loved him, and He must have felt sorrow as the young man turned away. Remember, Jesus had told him to sell all that he had, and then to give it to the poor and follow Him. The other disciples had left everything to follow Him. What was being taught? There is an inner clinging to, and putting first, which makes our words untrue when we say we love the Lord. The outside of the cup may seem clean, but inside many things are placed before the Lord in our love and concern. The disciples are very discouraged when Jesus says: "Children, how hard it is to enter the kingdom of God! It is easier for a camel to go through the eye of a needle than for a rich man to enter the kingdom of God" (Mark 10:24). You remember, the disciples asked among themselves, "Who then can be saved?" It seemed impossible! It became harshly revealing that they couldn't be sure that inside themselves they had totally put the Lord first. Who could be saved under such stringent circumstances and requirements of perfection? Then came Jesus' reply, "With man this is impossible, but not with God; all things are possible with God" (Mark 10:27).

> Peter said to him, "We have left everything to follow you!" "I tell you the truth," Jesus replied, "no one who has left home or brothers or sisters or mother or father or children or fields for me and the gospel will fail to receive a hundred times as much in this present age (homes, brothers, sisters, mothers, children and fields—and with them, persecutions) and in the age to come, eternal life. But many who are first will be last, and the last first." (Mark 10:28-31)

Such titanic things are being opened up to us by Jesus here. There is the need of wholehearted love and putting the Lord first, so that nothing can get in the way. No human being can be this wholehearted, and the rich, whether in material things or in family relationships, will find it harder, yes impossible, to turn complete-ly away from these and to the Lord. If it were not for the grace of God in providing the way for broken commandments to be for-given, through the payment Christ made on the cross, then not one of us could be saved. With God, this impossibility has been made possible.

Jesus then goes on to link turning from the enormous wealth the young man had with turning away from family, mother and father, lands, etc. He completes the teaching by saying that nothing is left for the Lord's sake without His giving back far more in this life, to say nothing of eternal life in the glorious perfection that is ahead. It fits right in with the teaching that if we seek first the kingdom of

God, all these things will be added to us—all the things we daily need to answer Who am I? and What will fulfill me? It fits right in with the exchange of losing life in order to find life.

We have been given a possibility of proving the *reality*, in a measure, that we are trusting the Lord enough to turn from the seen riches to the unseen riches that are ahead of us, and also that we are trusting the Creator of all the beauty of the universe to be fair in what He is asking. Jesus makes clear that loving the Lord, turning from family and lands, puts us in the place of having a bottomless barrel of love to give, plenty for father and mother and all the rest of our relations, a hundredfold in fact, and many more people to love.

When you come from this context, constantly remembering the fifth commandment to honor and respect father and mother, and then turn to Luke 14:25-27, it is easier to recognize and feel the impact, which comes as a shock but which spells out the cost of being a clean cup inside. We can again imagine the twisted inhuman look of the Punks on the outside; our concern is not to look like that to God on the inside! We need not be afraid of being a caricature of a human being if we follow the commands of God.

> Large crowds were traveling with Jesus, and turning to them he said, "If anyone comes to me and does not hate his father and mother, his wife and children, his brothers and sisters—yes, even his own life—he cannot be my disciple. And anyone who does not carry his cross and follow me cannot be my disciple."

Jesus goes on to speak of counting the cost when you are building a building or preparing for war, and then once more says:

> "In the same way, any of you who does not give up everything he has cannot be my disciple. Salt is good, but if it lose its saltiness, how can it be made salty again? It is fit neither for the soil nor for the manure pile; it is thrown out. He that has ears to hear, let him hear."

This Jesus is our Lord and Savior, our tender Shepherd and our loving Master, our Substitute who loved us enough to die in our place. He is spelling out some of the ingredients of perfection! He, the perfect One who says, "Be ye perfect as my Father in heaven is perfect," is now spelling out some of the ingredients which would have to be included, in perfectly following the Lord, in perfectly trusting Him, in perfectly loving Him. He is speaking to those who all too easily and glibly are saying as they crowd around Him, "I'll follow You." He is saying, "You have no idea of what following me costs. It costs everything you have and count precious, putting the Creator, the living God, the King of kings, the Prince of Peace, the Everlasting Father as really first in every aspect within your being."

This Jesus is making crystal clear that the rich young ruler is autonomous, that he is putting himself first and putting his possessions first. He is also making it clear that others are in danger of putting their mothers and fathers first, their families first.

He is not changing the fifth commandment to honor and respect mother and father, even if one is turning away from the false base the mother and father are living on. He is not changing the command to love each other, nor is he denying the essence of that love as described in 1 Corinthians 13: "Love is patient, love is kind. . . . It always protects, always trusts, always hopes, always perseveres. Love never fails." Jesus is not changing the admonition to always follow the way of love. He is simply making dazzlingly clear the facts about how total our love of God is meant to be—out of which comes some reality of love for each other.

The fifth commandment is the first of the commandments dealing with how we are to treat other human beings with love! The first place we have to exhibit that is with the father and mother we have by birth or by adoption.

What a marvelous balance we are given to bring us understanding!

6: THE SIXTH COMMANDMENT

I was sitting in a dentist's chair at the University of Pennsylvania's Dental School's practical clinic. Young dentists were getting their quota of fillings and specific kinds of dental work done. My student dentist was using my teeth to get his hammered gold fillings ticked off his list of requirements; so I had the only two hammered gold fillings I was ever to have done, right then! They are still intact by the way, and that was forty-four years ago; so the headache that came from the tap, tap, tap, was worth it! We were in Fran's second year in seminary, and Priscilla was on the way. I'll never forget the excitement of the moment, when in that dentist chair surrounded by fifty other people sitting in chairs getting dental work done inexpensively, suddenly I felt another faint tap, this time in my abdomen! I held my breath in secret excitement. My very first feeling of a life within me . . . somebody I didn't know yet had made me aware that "Heshe" (our name for the baby whose gender we didn't know yet) was making movements I could feel.

Life! What a mystery! Tiny cells, tiny chromosomes, multiplying to make a person so full of talents and personality that now after knowing Prisca for forty-four years I am still getting to know her. Consider the marvel of personality and whole persons made up of so many factors, human beings with a potential of existing forever, and of diverse creative skills only hindred by the fall. How can you describe life? How can I? We know only that little bit that we discover in our short years of living since we first made that movement our own mothers felt. How can we really know what life means in full until we have our new bodies which will be hindered no longer, and which will not die. It is the constant presence of death that spoils the understanding of life! It was not meant to be so.

What a tragedy that the fall took place, and that death came as a result. I wonder how long it took Adam and Eve to understand exactly what physical death meant. They experienced separation from God—in spiritual death—as soon as they left the garden, never to know that walking and talking face to face again. Their separation from each other and their strains and stresses as a married couple, and the strains and stresses that came with their children, were experienced constantly as days and months and years went on. But death? The real understanding of death, the separation of body from spirit, did not come for years, and then only as they experienced total separation from Abel, but not yet the experience of their own death.

The first death was the result of a killing, a direct murder in anger. It must have come as a shock to Cain, as well as to Adam and Eve. A human being's body, not breathing, not speaking, growing cold, was something no one had seen before. Understanding must have come slowly and agonizingly, and the realization must have come back in terrible shock waves. In a way every person's experience of death in the family or death taking place among a circle of friends is the same unbelievable shock. Yet, there must have been a very realistic need to discover how final death was when it was the first time it had ever taken place.

The human race has turned away from God so thoroughly that at the time of Noah an opportunity for them was given for a period of years, during which Noah built the ark, to discover what God was saying to them, and to turn to Him in belief. They had an opportunity to demonstrate that belief by coming into the ark with Noah before the flood came. However, the jeering and violent unbelief was so complete that no one but Noah's family paid any attention to the warning that a flood would cover the earth, and the population was wiped out. Only Noah was left, and those with him in the ark.

It was after the flood was over, after Noah had offered the prescribed sacrifices to God, that He made the beautiful promise never again to destroy the whole human race at once:

> "Never again will I curse the ground because of man, even though the inclination of his heart is evil from childhood. And never again will I destroy all living creatures, as I have done.
>> As long as the earth endures,
>> seedtime and harvest,
>> cold and heat,
>> summer and winter,
>> day and night
>> will never cease." (Genesis 8:21, 22)

In the midst of making this promise, this covenant, with the first gorgeous rainbow sealing the promise, God spoke strongly concerning the responsibility each person had for the life of his fellow men.

> "And from each man, too, I will demand an accounting for the life of his fellow man.
>> Whoever sheds the blood of a man,
>> by man shall his blood be shed;
>> for in the image of God
>> has God made man.
> As for you, be fruitful and increase in number; multiply on the earth and increase upon it." (Genesis 9:5-7)

This very first command to not kill, with the penalty of death for a death to demonstrate the preciousness of life, was given in the context of the command to have babies, who would be of course these human beings increasing in number, made in the image of God, precious to Him, having value in history.

Not only was the command given to be fruitful and multiply, but so often the picture of utter emptiness is spoken of as barren, as with a "barren womb," in many places in the Bible. In the Bible, birth is used to picture the entrance into the family of the living God, the company of believers forever. Birth is a beginning that is meant to have a continuity with life of a certain length on earth, and the new birth indicates a spiritual birth into everlasting life.

The body one has when the forty-six chromosomes have multiplied and grown for nine months within one's mother and then have become ready to live outside is so precious that when death entered the world through the fall, God had already planned the marvelous forming of the body of Jesus within Mary for nine months so that He could live, and die, and rise again to open the way for our resurrection and eternal life in our bodies. It was the excruciatingly important matter of our having our bodies for all eternity—changed, but the same bodies raised again—which made Christ's resurrection as the firstfruit so important. His resurrected body was the firstfruit, ours will be among the fruit to follow. All our bodies will be like his resurrected body.

Are the forty-six chromosomes leading to the whole person important? How marvelous is the work of God in creating human beings who could reproduce, who could have children from their physical oneness, children who would have eternal life one day, but who would also become adults and form new families, form the next generation.

Children are a gift of the Lord, the Bible tells us over and over again, and to treat the priceless gift of their lives entrusted into our hands lightly or carelessly is horrible to contemplate. If human beings are held accountable for the life of their fellowmen, being held accountable for the life of one of these precious gifts is staggering!

Come to Psalm 127:3-5.

> Lo, children are a heritage of the Lord: and the fruit of the womb is his reward. As arrows are in the hand of a mighty man; so are children of the youth. Happy is the man that hath his quiver full of them: they shall not be ashamed, but they shall speak with the enemies in the gate. (KJV)

Think of priceless inventions such as telephones, cameras, typewriters, and sewing machines, and the difference they make in life. It is impossible to compare these with God's invention of human beings, made in His image to think and act and feel, to have ideas and choose, to be creative and love and communicate—and to reproduce. Each human being has potential for being involved in bringing a new being into existence. How awful to treat a new human being as a kind of counterfeit piece of matter that isn't of any value at all. But even more, how terrible it is to forget that God the Creator has said that children are an inheritance, and a reward of His, given as a good gift.

> Blessed is every one that feareth the Lord; that walketh in his ways. For thou shalt eat the labor of thine hands: happy shalt thou be, and it shall be well with thee. Thy wife shall be as a fruitful vine by the sides of thine house; thy children like olive plants round about thy table. Behold, that thus shall the man be blessed that feareth the Lord. . . . Yea, thou shalt see thy children's children, and peace upon Israel. (Psalm 128:1-4, 6, KJV)

This picture the Psalmist gives to be sung with fervent voices and to be as a "hit song" upon the lips of the Israelites, and ours, is one evidence of a fulfilled life showing forth the answer to the question Who am I? I am one involved with life, life in the form of generations, caring for each other, bound together in a day-by-day communication, seeing each other, exchanging ideas in conversation, handing down traditions, but most importantly, making truth known to the next generation. Physical life is a precious commodity. Out of it comes the sweetness of the Beethoven Piano Trios, with a violin, cello, and piano bringing forth gorgeous waterfalls of music flowing not only over the ears of the listener, but through the whole "sounding" board of the physical system—made by God to respond to music as well as to hear it! In today's society, it is likely Beethoven would have been aborted. Our society does nothing to protect even the normal unborn life, and he had a succession of abnormal older brothers and sisters and unlikely family genes. In order for me to be hearing this music at this moment, not only did Beethoven have to be born, but Edison had to be born too, to start the whole thing of the phonograph, so that the Beaux Arts Trio can sit in New York and perfectly throw their talents and personalities into performing Beethoven trios nonstop for pressed records to bring them to—how many? Physical life—the mystery of the genes bringing forth another generation, God's "blessing," we are told. Human life is not something easily obtained. It is strong, but frail, and so easily taken away.

God who created human life—who knows what myriad capacities physical life has—is the only One who has absolute laws which continue to be the basis for physical life. He alone knows the total capacity of what He has made.

His law, His Ten Commandments, are worth finding out about, meditating upon, talking about, and attempting to put into practice. We need to listen to Him speaking to Noah. We need to stand beside Noah in all the freshness of the world after the flood, in the light of the rainbow, and hear the command that warns first of all that there is to be an accounting. There will be an account to settle up for every human being. One factor that will enter into that accounting is the seriousness of murder: anyone who commits murder must pay the cost with his own life. Coupled with that serious warning is the command to have children, making the begetting of life the opposite command to the cutting off of a life.

The close coupling of these two orders given by God to Noah as the civilization started afresh certainly points up the horror of accepting the murder of the innocent unborn people as is done in abortion. Of course, as people multiplied and again turned from God to the false gods and idols of their own imaginations, the killing of babies soon came to be a part of their false worship. But for those who remained faithful to the true God, babies, from the moment of conception, were counted as a priceless gift.

As we come to the sixth commandment, standing to hear Moses read it immediately after his reading the commandment which had to do with the primary relationship of honoring father and mother, we need to understand it in succession, in context. People so very often isolate the commandments and begin to argue in the context where they want to place them without listening to God's Word and letting it speak.

Remember, the commandments as given in Exodus 20 start with "And God spoke all these words: . . ." Then comes the sixth: "You shall not murder."

Since unborn babies are the youngest in the human family, the youngest human beings who are alive, it is really logical to think of them first. No one can be murdered if he or she is not alive. To kill anyone, to stop the heart from beating, to stop the blood from circulating, the person has to be alive. It would be impossible to murder someone who was not alive. We need to think about the beginning of life, as well as the potential of life (such as in musicians), to have a background to talk about murdering. The murder of an unborn baby is the murder of a potential Beethoven or a potential member of the Beaux Arts Trio, as well as a potential farmer, baker, or candlestick maker. Each one is meant to be woven together with others to fulfill their needs and potentialities and to enable others to have a place in the community of human beings.

Idealistic? No, this is what was meant to be—always remembering that we live in an abnormal world, a spoiled world, and things are not as they were meant to be. Nevertheless we have a pattern, a standard, a set of commandments which are to help us get back on the solid rock of reality instead of sliding around in a bog of mud that leads to a patch of quicksand. Human beings hanging out their shingles to let it be known that their chosen job is to help kill babies before they are born is simply *not* what human beings were made to do in order to have a satisfying, rich and full life. To have the killing of unknown Beethovens and Helen Kellers as one's career and creative work is like having the tearing down of art museums as one's fulfillment of a yearning for beauty! We will always be affected by the pattern of "the scarecrow." If we have a career of breaking one of the Ten Commandments, we begin to be like Punks inside.

Aborting life, snuffing out tiny, growing people, murdering boys and girls of all nationalities, burning and destroying perfect little hearts, fingers and toes, brains and ears, vocal chords and wee feet, all just weeks away from being able to be washed, clothed, fed, cuddled, and affected for a lifetime by a warm and loving welcome into the world—what a career!

There are those who counsel people who are sad, broken, fearful, unhappy, full of guilt, without a base for life, seeking some sort of fulfillment and freedom by telling them, "Just kill your little baby, the grandchild of your parents and the cousin of your brother's children, just kill it, and go on without remembering what happened. Forget it, and be free to go on and enjoy your own body without that growing tumor inside of you. Be free to enjoy life alone, without ever hearing your own child's voice or seeing whether her eyes are blue or brown, her hair curly or straight, her talents for ballet or violin, her mind mathematical or philosophical. Forget it—you won't wake up in the night crying; that's just a lot of old wives' tales."

To give that kind of false counsel is to be sliding into the lies Satan would have people believe about themselves and becoming the mouthpiece for them. "You aren't really a mother. You won't feel like a mother. That was just a piece of tissue, something like marmalade, in you. It's just like having a splinter taken out." What false counseling! What an example of the blind leading the blind! Each person who counsels someone to kill, to murder, the relative inside her own body is violating the sixth commandment, but also violating the fifth. We are to care for our relatives, or we are worse than infidels, and we are not to murder. So in an abortion two commandments are broken at once, two specifically.

In the tenth Psalm one can feel the strength of emotion we should have for the innocent girls or young women being given wrong or wicked advice, as well as for the innocent babies who if they could sing would sing, "Mama, Mama, Mama, don't believe their lies. Please let me look into your eyes. Mama, Mama, Mama, don't leave me" (From "Too Young to Die," by Dallas Graham).

> In his arrogance the wicked man hunts down the weak,
>   who are caught in the schemes he devises.
> He boasts of the cravings of his heart,
>   he blesses the greedy and reviles the Lord. . . .
> He says to himself, "Nothing will shake me;
>   I'll always be happy and never have trouble."
> His mouth is full of curses and lies and threats;
>   trouble and evil are under his tongue.
> He lies in wait near the villages;
>   from ambush he murders the innocent,
>   watching in secret for his victims.
> He lies in wait like a lion in cover;
>   he lies in wait to catch the helpless. . . .
> He says to himself, "God has forgotten;
>   he covers his face and never sees."
>
>   (Psalm 10:2, 3, 6-9, 11)

What a picture of today—not just the violence of terrorists hiding in every kind of ambush to surprise victims in their own homes or places of business, but a picture of the pouncing on the unborn and dragging them out of hiding to be destroyed before they can ever ask, Who am I? and How can I be fulfilled? And what is more, so many, many times the mother is not given a chance to find out the answers either.

The anguished cry—"Oh, I wish I hadn't! Why didn't someone *tell* me I'd feel like this? No one explained to me that I'd dream of babies and wake up crying. No one told me I'd feel so empty"—is a cry that ought to be recorded for the people who are promising freedom—freedom physically, intellectually, morally, emotionally, psychologically and spiritually. Freedom for the whole person? And what about the one who gave the other half of the forty-six chromosomes . . . the father, the other parent of the dead child? The destruction has wiped out his own son or daughter before he could feel his arms around his neck or hear him ask a question. A generation wiped out. The blessing God had promised now never to be experienced.

Human beings have been made by God to have family relationships. In today's abnormal world many are cut off from this joy because of the spoiledness and sin that has come in to separate people. But to murder the next generation is to add guilt to loneliness as the years go on. The sin of murder and of not caring at all about one's relatives brings with it a penetrating effect in this life which needs to be dealt with.

Jeremiah speaks to the Israelites, but also to those who call themselves Christians today and feel that they are really the people of God. It is a word of warning from God.

This is the word that came to Jeremiah from the Lord: "Stand at the gate of the Lord's house and there proclaim this message: 'Hear the word of the Lord, all you people of Judah who come through these gates to worship the Lord. This is what the Lord Almighty, the God of Israel says: Reform your ways and your actions, and I will let you live in this place. Do not trust in deceptive words and say, "This is the temple of the Lord, the temple of the Lord, the temple of the Lord!" If you really change your ways and your actions and deal with each other justly, if you do not oppress the alien, the fatherless or the widow and do not shed innocent blood in this place, and if you do not follow other gods to your harm, then I will let you live in this place, in the land I gave your forefathers for ever and ever. But look, you are trusting in deceptive words that are worthless.

" 'Will you steal and murder, commit adultery and perjury, burn incense to Baal and follow other gods you have not known, and then come and stand before me in this house, which bears my Name, and say, "we are safe"—safe to do all these detestable things? Has this house, which bears my Name, become a den of robbers to you? But I have been watching! declares the Lord.' " (Jeremiah 7:1-11)

Those who call themselves God's people, whether Protestants or Catholics or Jews, whether evangelicals or liberals, whether charismatics or those who have a rigid form of worship—are all in danger of "trusting in deceptive words," in danger of saying words which are devoid of meaning, because of actions making it clear that the words are only a kind of outside paint job, covering up detestable things inside. Just saying "this is God's house," "this is a worship service," "praise the Lord," "we are praising God," "bless my soul," and other phrases of worship does nothing. God listens only if the Word of God is being really believed and honored and lived by. Go back and read the list again as God enumerates the things that are detestable to Him. He sees into the lives and actions, as well as into the minds and hearts, of each congregation of people saying, "We are safe because we are saying the right words." The list is frightening because we all can find ourselves described.

As we think of the sixth commandment now, that murder is forbidden, we see around us today the shedding of innocent blood in abortion, at every stage of life *before* birth, in allowing babies to starve to death *after* they are born if there is something wrong which the doctor thinks would make life "not worth living." The door is also open to euthanasia, the killing of the mentally ill, senile, or just old, for growing numbers of reasons, including economic reasons.

So very many religious people, including many who profess to be believing Christians who want to live by the Bible, think that they are not bound by God's severe word concerning murder when they shrug their shoulders about abortion, infanticide, and euthanasia. They act as if it is something Christians, believers, can differ about, like music, or what kind of a bell the church is going to have.

Another lie is the evaluation of human life as having to come up to a certain measurable standard to be "life worth living." If we were to compare the best person alive today with what human beings would be like had there been no fall, what "normal" was like without any imperfections, not one person would have a "quality of life worthy to be lived." Thank God He has told us that we have a purpose now, even though the creation has been devastated and we are so spoiled. And thank God He has told us that one day we shall all be restored, and our new bodies will be our experience of reality—forever. Then we will know what perfection is like. The waiting period, as we live now, is to be an important one, as well as a busy one, whatever our handicaps are. Murder is not the way to care for each other's problems and afflictions!

Recently in an English seminar for *Whatever Happened to the Human Race?* a doctor stood up in the audience and told of how her own little girl was born with spinal bifida and of how she and her husband (also a doctor) read on her chart that she was to be given no care, no medication, and no food by mouth. She was being starved to death on the decision of some doctor or doctors that her life was not worthy to be lived. This couple kidnapped their own baby and took her home from that hospital, cared for her, gave her antibiotics when she was ill, loved and fed her, did all they could without the operation which had been refused them by social medicine. The little girl still needs that operation, but at two is beautiful in spite of being paralyzed from the waist down, is very bright and talkative, and a joy to her parents as well as a happy child.

What else can allowing a baby to starve to death, to become dehydrated because of the removal of all liquid, be called except murder? And who is guilty? As Christians, are we concerned and asking the Lord what He would have us do in this moment of history as standards swiftly slide from an absolute base to a relative one, changing with all the winds of opinions blowing from every side?

Suicide is another kind of murder—the murder of oneself rather than of another person. Of course, sudden mental breakdown, a demented mind, temporary insanity, can cause such swift action that time to reconsider is lost. God knows the heart, and He also knows all forms of illness and breakdown in the mind and emotions that can take place. God knows our strains and stresses and weakness. He tells of the varying weaknesses of His children and warns us to care for the weaker brother. People who are easily hit by temptation often are hit by a diversity of temptation, and the stronger should help the weaker, whatever the weakness may be. Care must be taken not to push anyone else into a place of temptation.

Certainly the whole movement of writing books and telling people *how* to commit suicide rather than going on with old age or cancer or whatever is something that must be fought by Christians. We are responsible for letting it be known that suicide is murder—and that the sixth commandment has not been canceled out. It is still one of God's absolutes. We are responsible to let it be known that there is no such thing as "sin with dignity"!

We each are tempted in different areas. Isaiah 5:20-23 describes a diversity of areas in which we need to confess horrible deeds to the Lord and ask for help not to do them again.

> Woe to those who call evil good
>   and good evil,
> who put darkness for light
>   and light for darkness,
> who put bitter for sweet
>   and sweet for bitter.
> Woe to those who are wise in their own eyes
>   and clever in their own sight.
> Woe to those who are heroes at drinking wine
>   and champions at mixing drinks,
> who acquit the guilty for a bribe,
>   but deny justice to the innocent.

In many countries where statistics number so and so many Christians, there is only a tiny minority who ever come out of the woodwork to make clear that they recognize that what is being done in their countries, their states, their cities or villages, their small communities, or even their churches or assemblies is directly contrary to the Word of God. It is even contrary to the basic Ten Commandments He gave to show people how to live.

For a believer who claims to be in God's family, either to help people to murder without it hurting their consciences, or to shrug one's shoulders and say, "It doesn't matter; we can differ on these subjects," is to be placing oneself in the Judge's chair and remaking the laws upon which to base the judgment.

So often human beings feel they are better than God. When they cannot understand all that God has commanded, they draw up another set of rules, and feel pious about it too, thinking their rules are not only better, but more compassionate and full of love. What twisted love! What twisted compassion! What lack of trust!

Long, long before Moses stood reading the Ten Commandments, God had made clear to the family of Noah as they began a new period of history that because people are made in the image of God and have such importance, when anyone murders another person, then the murderer is to die. Capital punishment was ordered by God to make clear the preciousness of life. The emphasis is direct and complete: the murderer is to die in the place of the murdered one, to show the sinfulness of the sin of snuffing out human life. The reason is, "for in the image of God has God made man." That was reason enough.

When we come to the time of Moses, the clear command, "You shall not murder," was explicitly widened in what came right after that. For instance in Exodus 21, the next chapter, explanations are given as to punishments for breaking this commandment. "Anyone who strikes a man and kills him shall surely be put to death." It is made clear that if this is done unintentionally, then there is a great difference, and he may flee to a place of refuge.

Note carefully: it took a death for a death when Christ died for us. The penalty for the worst sins was death. We have committed the worst sins in one way and another. And death *has* paid the price! Until we see that, we can't understand the total meaning of the death of Christ. It was capital punishment. Really so. But as the Son of God, the Lamb of God, the Savior, the Messiah, the King of kings, He could die in the place of so many! He, as infinite, could take the place of so very many finite ones. The only infinite One is God. Jesus as the I AM made it clear He could die in the place of all who would believe and bow and accept what He was doing for them, as well as making it clear He would rise again, and demonstrate that those for whom He died could also have the glorious hope of resurrection.

Can't you see, capital punishment is what the death of Jesus is all

about. It is for us He died! He took that punishment. He didn't say
with a shrug, "It's all right. Go ahead and sin by breaking all the
commandments. It's all right. Just live peaceful lives and turn your
backs on what others do. When wickedness increases, just shut
your eyes." No, Jesus said:

> "Do not think I have come to abolish the Law or the Prophets; I have
> not come to abolish them but to fulfill them. I tell you the truth, until
> heaven and earth disappear, not the smallest letter, not the least stroke
> of a pen, will by any means disappear from the Law until everything is
> accomplished. Anyone who breaks one of the least of these command-
> ments and teaches others to do the same will be called least in the
> kingdom of heaven, but whoever practices and teaches these com-
> mands will be called great in the kingdom of heaven. For I tell you that
> unless your righteousness surpasses that of the Pharisees and the
> teachers of the law, you will certainly not enter the kingdom of
> heaven." (Matthew 5:17-20)

This immediately precedes the very next words Jesus said as He
was sitting on a mountainside teaching the people who were
crowded there, with a diversity of open or shut minds, listening.

> "You have heard it was said to the people long ago, 'Do not murder,
> and anyone who murders will be subject to judgment.' [Note here that
> Jesus puts the two things together, murder and the capital punishment
> for that act.] But I tell you that anyone who is angry with his brother
> will be subject to judgment. [What judgment? Jesus is comparing
> anger which is strong enough anger to kill in one's mind, to murder.
> We can commit murder in our heads when we are angry. This Jesus
> says is worthy of the strong judgment for a committed murder—not by
> another human being, but by God.]
>
> "Again, anyone who says to his brother, 'Raca,' is answerable to the
> Sanhedrin. ["Raca" is an Aramaic term of contempt, and the Sanhedrin
> had a penalty for using it.] But anyone who says, 'You fool!' will be in
> danger of the fire of hell."

What is Jesus saying? He is communicating clearly that the kind
of anger that is within us when we say "you fool" is the kind of
anger that is murder in our thoughts. He is saying that civil law
may have its punishments, but that God's law when broken puts
people in danger of hell. God will not look the other way. Breaking
His law is serious.

We need to go back and cry with the disciples when Jesus spoke of how impossible it would be for a rich man to turn away from his great material possessions to put God first. We need to cry, "Who then *can* be saved? If our thoughts are akin to murder, and hell is the 'capital punishment' for such sin, who then *can* be saved?"

The answer is that with man it is impossible, but with God all things are possible. God has provided the substitute, the capital punishment which only Jesus could take in our place. The punishment has already been taken. It can accrue to us if we believe God as He tells us this amazing provision has been made for us and accept it. Fantastic love! Amazing grace! Stunning compassion! But at what a cost!

In 1 John 3, John is talking about love being a mark of the Christian and that which should make believers different from unbelievers. Among all that is given in this chapter, this particularly fits in right here:

> Do not be like Cain, who belonged to the evil one and murdered his brother. And why did he murder him? Because his own actions were evil and his brother's were righteous. Do not be surprised, my brothers, if the world hates you. We know that we have passed from death to life, because we love our brothers. [An evidence we can see in ourselves after we have accepted Christ as Savior is the evidence of a growing love that comes for others in the same family!] Anyone who does not love remains in death. Anyone who hates his brother is a murderer, and you know that no murderer has eternal life in him. This is how we know what love is: Jesus Christ laid down his life for us. And we ought to lay down our lives for our brothers. If anyone has material possessions and sees his brother in need but has no pity on him, how can the love of God be in him? Dear children, let us not love with words or tongue but with actions and in truth. (vv. 12-18)

True, we cannot keep the commandments well enough to earn our salvation. True, forgiveness is given on the basis of the perfect life of Christ and His death in our place, His taking the capital punishment that belonged to us. But after we have become God's children, something is meant to be different about us, and that something is meant to be shown by actions and deeds in line with the truth. In our growing Christian lives we should be coming closer to keeping the commandments of God, by the help of the

Holy Spirit. We should also be helping others to know what they consist of and how important they are. Surely, to encourage murder is not a part of the Christian life.

Then, just as we are about to reconsider our own lives and thoughts and actions, and to thank God that our situation is not hopeless, but that He has given hope, and a solution for each of us personally, suddenly one jumps up and says, "Hey, what about war?"

What about war?

First, the Bible is clear that the same God who commanded, "You shall not murder" also told His Old Testament people that they were to wage war. The people they fought were nations which had come to a place of a fullness of wickedness that demanded immediate judgment. At the time of Noah, God used the flood to judge those who had so completely turned away from him into wickedness. At the time of Sodom and Gomorrah, God destroyed the cities because the wickedness was total. In the battles which God commanded His people to wage, they were being used as His instrument of judgment when those about them had come to a fullness of wickedness. Prophecy in the New Testament makes clear that judgment is ahead. One day there will be a final battle before true and lasting peace will be ushered in. That final battle is described in the book of Revelation.

No one who takes the Bible as the authority from God can say that war has always been a breaking of the commandment "You shall not murder."

Christians have differed through the centuries as to whether there should be any war during the time between Christ's death and the last battle. We are told to turn the other cheek personally, but whether this extends to the national level is something Christians can differ on. In a fallen world there is a problem involving nations. The State is called upon to bring forth justice in a world that requires police forces to do this in each nation. This inward protection of each country extends to the borders. And the protection takes a variety of forms.

Within a country, and at the border of countries, there is continually a question of responsibility, and the facing of the question, Am I my brother's keeper? When a Christian sees a brutal man abusing a small child, and that man will not listen to reason, at some point the Christian with compassion and love for his neighbor, in this case the child, must do what he would if the child were his own and intervene with force.

Since the time of the Old Testament we have not had God commanding an individual war for judgment, nor His choosing a nation to represent Him. In a fallen world there can be all kinds of rationalization and manipulation, especially in a day of mass communication. However, there are cases where there is no other way to stop horrible injustices, mass murder, oppression, including torture, aggression and all the rest, except by war. We are far enough away from the war with Hitler's Germany now to judge it with some objectivity. Realizing what was happening there, one could ask how Christian love could possibly do nothing when we are told that "love always protects," "love never fails." If a nation such as the United States could intervene, how could it stand by and watch without attempting to help those crying out for help? Of course, no one can have the kind of certainty that the Old Testament people had when God specifically commanded them to go to war and laid out the strategy as with Gideon, but in a fallen world such a situation as Hitler's Germany calls forth strenuous action.

If we had been the ones in power in the countries which could help, and we knew in detail all that was going on in Hitler's Germany, could we have sunned ourselves in peaceful gardens and fields, on beaches or in mountain resorts, sending messages to those in Germany such as "Stand fast against the atrocities even at the cost of your lives" while we continued to enjoy our personal peace? Would we not have to intervene with force when all other means had failed?

War is complicated, and so is a police force, because people are complicated and sinful, and there are so many kinds of mixed motives as well as individually sinful acts. However, recognizing the complications does not change the fact that there comes a time for nations, as well as for the police force and for individuals, to intervene on the behalf of people who are being harmed, as well as for judgment.

This does not mean there will not be tears, nor does it mean that individual Christians do not have to face a decision about whether or not they can support any particular war. Naturally, as with all other situations in this spoiled world since the fall, there is no perfect nation and no perfect soldier. But Christians need to decide whether they can support the war they face. If not, they must be willing to say no, even at great personal cost. However, there will continue to be situations in a fallen world where such judgment and intervention will be needed, right up to the time when Christ Himself returns with justice to judge and fight the final battle.

Is it an easy decision to make? No. Never. And the reason why is always the same! The world is made up of imperfect people. However, in war, theoretically at least, those against whom the war is fought are those who have done something as a nation that is overwhelmingly wicked and who are continuing to do that which needs to be stopped. Other solutions failing, the extremity of war is demanded. In this kind of situation, war becomes its own kind of capital punishment on a larger scale. It is not simply a punishment; it is also a means of stopping an individual or nation from continuing in a "fullness of wickedness."

The One in whose image people were made, who says life is so precious that no human being is to murder another one without paying for that act with his own life, is one day going to put an end to all the wickedness which will have "filled the cup to overflowing" with the final battle. Satan, the liar who brought death and murder into the creation of God to devastate it, will be vanquished, and the victory will be complete.

> I saw heaven standing open and there before me was a white horse, whose rider is called Faithful and True. With justice he judges and makes war. His eyes are like blazing fire, and on his head are many crowns. He has a name written on him that no one but he himself knows. He is dressed in a robe dipped in blood, and his name is the Word of God. The armies of heaven were following him, riding on white horses and dressed in fine linen, white and clean. Out of his mouth comes a sharp sword with which to strike down the nations. "He will rule them with an iron scepter." He treads the winepress of the fury of the wrath of God Almighty. On his robe and on his thigh he has this name written: KING OF KINGS AND LORD OF LORDS. (Revelation 19:11-16)

Yes, an end is coming to murder, an end is coming to killing. Listen to 1 Corinthians 15:24-26. This comes right after we have been told that as in Adam all die, so in Christ all will be made alive: "Then the end will come, when he hands over the kingdom to God the Father after he has destroyed all dominion, authority and power. For he must reign until he has put all his enemies under his feet. The last enemy to be destroyed is death."

Then in Revelation 21:4 we are given a glimpse of the new heaven and the new earth, where the promise is given: "He will wipe every tear from their eyes. There will be no more death or mourning or crying or pain, for the old order of things has passed away."

7: THE SEVENTH COMMANDMENT

Suppose you had been brought up in a house where all the windows had been broken long before your birth, and had not been replaced but glued together in zigzag cracks, so that you had always looked out at the world through distorted perspective. How could you judge the description someone might give you of what your view would be like seen through crystal-clear glass with no drips of glue, and none of the myriad cracks?

A wistful little boy of seven whose parents had been divorced three times, and whose mixed-up list of homes included a bewildering number of grandparents and parents, sighed deeply as he confided to a friend's mother, "I just can't wait to grow up so that I can have a home of my own."

Two little girls in a Swiss boarding school were discussing what they would do when they grew up. The ten-year-old said firmly, "Well, I'm going to stay married for ten years the first time I get married, then I'll try a lot of different husbands."

A panel of social workers and teachers were discussing on television whether it was a breach of confidence to tell mothers when their little girls of nine were coming to them for contraceptives.

"Sex education includes descriptive movies which teach homosexual and lesbian sex as well as heterosexual sex, all in a factual setting, making no recommendations. Can you imagine? I couldn't believe what I was seeing could be meant for education of minors in school!" This was a doctor speaking, a sophisticated doctor who travels the world, not a small town farmer's wife.

"Yes," said the young professional man, "the judge gave the children to my wife." A common enough sorrow? Sadly so, but this situation has a different twist, since the woman who had left her husband had married another woman.

Not only does a husband come home to find a note saying, "I am leaving you," but the children come home to find that mom has left. And when they go to talk it over with friends in school, it is as common as telling of the last drilling in a dentist's chair. Just one of the disturbing things of life. Mothers? Fathers? Here today, gone tomorrow!

A Swiss doctor giving mothers advice on a radio program tells of the very basic need of supplying daughters with birth control pills in their handbags. "Never should you let your daughter go out after she is thirteen without having her birth control pills because things are not like they used to be when you were in school." And Switzerland is years behind the United States and some other countries in these areas.

Sweden takes pride that there is no distinction between married couples and couples who live together without being married. All the benefits are the same, including alimony if there is a separation. A strange rash of marriages has been taking place recently with couples who have lived together as much as eight years suddenly wanting something more in continuity and stability, so they turn to a wedding, with smiling children standing in front as flower girls or ring-bearers. Mother and daddy are getting married!

Then there are the marriage swapping parties going on in neighborhoods, and the communal marriages where children can't claim any one father, and the "cracked and glued glass" which the television presents as a window to what life is all about.

When you get done with a realistic look around at today's society, you begin to recognize why even Christians are beginning to fail to see the true answers to Who am I? and What will fulfill me?

Have you ever tried to describe a whole panorama of mountains as they look when the air is crystal clear and the sun has just set, coloring them all rosy pink, while the sky turns a powder blue and the full moon slithers up behind the peaks to add its breathtaking copper sphere to the other beauty? Have you tried to describe this during a fog and slashing rain when even the trees across the field cannot be seen? You wave a hand and say, "Right there is where the Dents du Midi are, and then there is the Diablerets, and in that place over there the moon comes up while the afterglow of the sun is still an amazing pink on the snow." Your arm has pointed to dull grey, to streaks of rain, to a monochromatic color scheme. If the person standing beside you has never been in the Swiss Alps before and has nothing to relate to what you are saying because he lives on a flat plain, you need to use very careful description indeed to make yourself understood.

In the mishmash of today's standards of right and wrong, many children are being born into an atmosphere that is alien to the Ten Commandments, so alien that to simply state them would have no meaning at all. What can unclean mean when a person lives in mud and filth and has never seen anything but dirty rags for clothing? What could it possibly mean to a ragged child, covered with sores and flies, if you said, "keep clean"? But it isn't only true of children; many adults have lost all sight of any true perspective of alternatives to the way everyone around them is living.

Unhappily the Ten Commandments mean nothing at all to much of the world's population. What is even more depressing is that they mean very little to many who call themselves the people of God. The "cracked and glued together glass" has come to believers' homes too, and the warped view is affecting their judgment in answering Who am I? and What will fulfill me? The warped view forgets that God has made people and that He has made the rules in line with who they are, with who they *really* are.

The seventh commandment is this:
"You shall not commit adultery."
What is adultery? An explanation is needed.

Adultery is the smashing of a rare and mystical thing, a unity, a oneness between two people who have become one because of something which God made them to be capable of having together, which had the original purpose of making two people one. Read again Genesis 1:27, 2:24, 25.

So God created man in his own image, in the image of God he created him; male and female he created them. . . . For this reason a man will leave his father and mother and be united to his wife, and they will become one flesh. The man and his wife were both naked, and they felt no shame.

The original reason given for the physical oneness, the sexual act in marriage, is oneness.

God had created people, male and female, with a capacity for oneness with each other, a fruitful physical oneness that would bring forth another generation of people. God created people with a capacity for oneness in working together, communicating verbally, exchanging ideas, doing creative works, eating together, and "walking and talking with God in the cool of the evening." People were made in His image that they might have a three-way oneness, intellectually, spiritually, and physically on a horizontal level. People were made so that they could have a oneness with God spiritually, to love Him, worship Him, have communication with Him, and to be able to seek His counsel and advice and help day by day. These two onenesses have been set forth to us in His Word, the Bible, and have to do with our knowing who we are and what will fulfill us. It is not just a question of right and wrong; it is a question of what *is*. To act contrary to what is is to constantly bump one's head against a wall. We all do it in a variety of ways—and we all have bruises from the variety of walls we have hit!

The comparison of our being made to be able to have oneness with a human being and our being made to have oneness spiritually with God is made clear in various parts of the Bible, but one of the clearest is in Ephesians 5:25-33:

Husbands, love your wives, just as Christ loved the church and gave himself up for her to make her holy, cleansing her by the washing with water through the word, and to present her to himself as a radiant church, without stain or wrinkle or any other blemish, but holy and blameless. In this same way, husbands ought to love their wives as their own bodies. He who loves his wife loves himself. After all, no one ever hated his own body, but he feeds and cares for it, just as Christ does the church—for we are members of his body. "For this reason a man will leave his father and mother and be united to his wife, and the two will become one flesh." This is a profound mystery—but I am talking about Christ and the church. However, each one of you also must love his wife as he loves himself, and the wife must respect her husband.

What God said to Adam and Eve before the fall, quoted here so many centuries later, is still to be the way of life, still to be the preparation for a new generation, as well as a oneness for a lifetime. A father and mother are involved: a man and a woman have produced the man; and another father and mother are involved, another man and woman have produced the woman. Male and female! This is a basic fact as well as a basic law. Marriage between human beings means one male and one female—and a fruitful oneness. The oneness is the primary factor of their physical coming together; the fruit is an evidence of that oneness, not the primary reason for it. God speaks in this order of things when He talks to Adam and Eve, and the same thing is true centuries later when the New Testament is given.

Today's people are not only denying God's existence. They are denying their own existence by denying that there is any importance to the magnificent differences between the male and female, and by denying the wonderful possibility of oneness. Perfect? Not now. Not since the fall. There is no perfect male, no perfect female, no perfect oneness. Everything has been spoiled. There are no perfect relationships. But to try to deny and wipe out the differences between male and female, to try to live on the basis of something that does not exist, a neuter being, is to deny that there is any absolute answer to Who am I?

The beauty of the human relationship, which has such rich possibilities, is spoiled by all the drive to put self, ego, one's own fulfillment ahead of all else. This frantic search for happiness and fulfillment ensures brokenness and ugliness because it is the very opposite, in all its parts, of what people were created to be. Attempts to live on a false base of what it means to be human and to achieve total freedom end in a total freedom—from joy and from fulfillment! It doesn't work. People can't declare that it is fine to worship idols, to marry someone of the same sex, to live on the basis of drugs and disregard for any of the body's need for sleep or food, and end up with happy glowing faces, full of certainty as to their purpose in life. The Ten Commandments give an unchanging series of jolts to human beings through the centuries to bring them back from whatever new form of lies are being perpetrated as to what being human is all about, as to what life is all about, as to what fulfillment is all about.

"You shall not commit adultery," Moses read to the crowds of people who had just been committing the worst kind of adultery in turning *from* God, with whom they were meant to be one spiritually, *to* the golden calf, an idol with the word "God" etched upon it. Using language to cover up what was going on, they had been rationalizing the awful sin of turning to an idol by pretending to themselves it was God. In the accompanying orgy, they were carrying that adultery into their physical lives by turning to other people not their husbands or wives. This abominable mixture of spiritual adultery—placing other gods in the one true God's place in any human being's life or experience—with physical adultery—placing other human beings in the place of the one with whom one is joined by God as we are told—had been taking place right before the law was read from the tablets of stone!

"You shall have no other gods before me" had already been read. Now the law turns to our relationship with other human beings, and after telling about the relationship with mother and father, then comes the husband and wife and the strong command not to commit adultery by being unfaithful to each other. You are not to be unfaithful to God; and as you come together as couples you are not to be unfaithful to each other. The oneness on a finite, horizontal human level has great importance. It has an importance in fulfilling who you are and it has an importance in being a daily, constant picture throughout all history of the oneness between God and His people.

Years and years after Moses read that command, the example was going to be given of how similar the relationship is meant to be between Christ, who died for His Bride (the church), and between husband and wife. The husband is to love his wife and give himself to her in a deep and similar way. If husbands tried to copy in some tiny measure the amazing love Christ has for the church, and cared for their wives in some miniscule manner the way Christ cares for us as He opens the way to us for communication, and for making requests, and if wives respected and desired to please their husbands in a tiny manner, a small particle of the way we are meant to please and bring joy to Christ—then there would be no problems!

Faithfulness to God and faithfulness to husband and wife are both meant to be fulfilling. But they will only be fulfilling as we follow the teaching that God has been so careful to give us. It is the rebellion against living in the real world on the basis of who I am that brings the devastation.

People have separated sex from the oneness of two people, man and woman as husband and wife. They have done this through all history, just as they have separated worship and spirituality from oneness with the true eternal God, the I AM. The rebellion of mankind, human beings, has always existed in these two areas. Both are adultery.

The turning away from the worship of the Creator of all things, the Maker of heaven and earth, and turning to Baal or Molech not only involved horrible practices that were a travesty of true worship, such as the burning of babies, the sacrifice of young sons or daughters to be thrown from cliffs, the cutting of the flesh of worshipers and so on. It also involved a frenzied desire for feeling—bizarre at times, but spiritual feeling nonetheless. The terrific diversity of false worship, false gods, idol worship, and all the counterfeit forms of worship we have talked about in previous chapters have one thing in common—people get a feeling, an experience of spirituality, and seek for more and more of that feeling. It is all they can depend on, and it becomes an integration point. The feeling of spirituality a person gets in a cathedral with light coming through the rose window and an organ filling the air with marvelous music can also be totally false if the person does not believe in the existence of God at all, is not thinking of Him or communicating to Him, but simply sitting there bathed in a lovely warm feeling they would describe as spiritual.

People who are not God's people often describe the feeling of peace, quietness and spirituality they get in doing yoga, in sitting in certain shrines, in performing certain religious rites. And God's people, who have been having a hard time with the drudgery of daily work and a much-less-than-perfect preacher to listen to, and the lack of cultural rapport with their believing friends, and the frustrating lack of beauty or spirituality they had been wanting, suddenly become envious and feel cheated out of what they are missing and are tempted to go ahead and try whatever false worship is around. The false can be such a pleasing counterfeit that it can fool people, for a time. They can enjoy for a season the excitement of feeling what seems like the satisfying spiritual feelings they have longed for. And so they plunge into spiritual adultery with complete abandon!

People who are promiscuous in sex, sleeping with a diversity of others, describe the marvelous feelings they say are so satisfying. Others describe what ought to be felt and point out what people are missing if their experiences or feelings have not measured up. People state that their second or third marriages after divorce are so much better, and that one needs to try again to find sexual satisfaction. There are those who turn away to finding sexual excitement in homosexual or lesbian relationships, and declare that no one has understood what feeling can be like who has not been freed from "binding taboos," or from "outdated laws" of the past. There are those who seek excitement by going to prostitutes, or engaging in a mixture of highly prepared sex orgies, shows, parties, and bizarre substitutes for anything that they might term normal. The wildly frantic search before old age comes and it is too late drives people into wanting to experience everything of feeling that they have heard about. Adultery follows adultery, and the people whose marriage doesn't seem to bring a satisfying sexual feeling and has other drawbacks besides are tempted to try to find happiness, which they have become fooled into thinking is one of their basic rights. The whole atmosphere is so filled with babbling and tumult about the need to be fulfilled sexually that even Christians come to think they are being denied something that is their basic right and forget to look into God's Word for any direction concerning this part of life.

People throw away any possibility of finding out who they are until it is too late to live in the light of the answer. People throw away any possibility of being fulfilled until they have destroyed so much and have wasted so much of life that they haven't much time left to discover reality of fulfillment.

You see, continuity is a part of our oneness with other human beings, whether in the husband and wife relationship or in the family, and continuity is the everlasting part of our relationship with God. Continuity which goes on forever is needed to fulfill the person I am, the being of my existence. I am a person with a memory, with a capacity for growth and change in my intellectual life, my emotional life, my spiritual life, my creative life; and I need time and continuity to have the best conditions for being fulfilled. To break, splinter, shatter continuity is destructive to the development and fulfillment of who I am.

Now of course sin entered the world at the fall, and people have been twisted and spoiled ever since. No one is fully developed into what or who he or she could be, nor is anyone completely fulfilled. That will not exist until we have our new bodies at the return of Christ and all the shattered creation is restored. However, to turn away from what God has set forth as the basic rules of how to live in the light of what He has created is to turn away from *any* possibility of having a fraction of restoration in this life.

When Jesus had finished saying these things, he left Galilee and went into the region of Judea to the other side of the Jordan. Large crowds followed him, and he healed them there. Some Pharisees came to him to test him. They asked, "Is it lawful for a man to divorce his wife for any and every reason?"

"Haven't you read," he replied, "that at the beginning the Creator 'made them male and female,' and said, 'For this reason a man will leave his father and mother and be united to his wife, and the two will become one flesh'? So they are no longer two, but one. Therefore what God has joined together, let man not separate."

"Why then," they asked, "did Moses command that a man give his wife a certificate of divorce and send her away?"

Jesus replied, "Moses permitted you to divorce your wives because your hearts were hard. But it was not this way from the beginning. I tell you that anyone who divorces his wife, except for marital unfaithfulness, and marries another woman commits adultery."

The disciples said to him, "If this is the situation between a husband and wife, it is better not to marry."

Jesus replied, "Not everyone can accept this teaching, but only those to whom it has been given. For some are eunuchs because they were born that way; others were made that way by men; and others have renounced marriage because of the kingdom of heaven. The one who can accept this should accept it." (Matthew 19:1-12)

Jesus has strongly declared here that although Moses allowed divorce for that time, "it was not this way from the beginning." From the beginning God meant marriage to be a lasting relationship. Had there been no death, not only would we not be separated from our bodies, but we would not be separated from each other. Death to a relationship is not meant to be a part of fulfillment. Death to the continuity of a family is not meant to take place. Physical death separates even husband and wife. "Till death do us part" is a reminder of this on the very joyous occasion of making vows before God and God's people to be faithful to each other for a continuity of time. Physical death separates body and spirit. Death is not a pretty thing. It is a tearing apart of something that is meant to be whole, not splintered and torn. Divorce is an act of death to a relationship God says should not be separated.

Just as spiritual adultery separates us from God, physical adultery separates us from husband or wife. This is the only reason given for divorce—a deliberate unfaithfulness and breaking. But that turning away can be forgiven by God. As we ask forgiveness and come back to Him, He accepts us back—even when we have committed adultery in false worship—on the basis of the death of Christ in our place. So physical adultery can also be forgiven, and husband and wife can go on together, recognizing the frailty and spoiledness of human beings since the fall.

The increasing incidence of divorce among Christians is like an epidemic. Satan has thrown a blinding kind of dust in the air, it would seem, to keep us all from having the courage to consider the Word of God as serious and important to follow. "Be ye perfect as my Father in heaven is perfect" seems too impossible to attain, so the reality of the goal is shoved under the rug. "He that endures to the end" and all such admonitions are uncomfortable. The thing to do is simply sing, "I'm so happy," and to insist on finding happiness to the exclusion of anyone else, and to forget Paul's list of afflictions! No one seems to feel that it is important to work hard—whether in the face of persecutions, taunts of our neighbors, temptations dangling in front of us, or the afflictions of the flesh, such as a series of illnesses or shocks. But we must keep on working hard on our relationship with the Lord, and our relationships with each other, in marriage if we are married, in the family circle, among the people with whom we work, so that the world may have evidence that there is a reality to our being the Lord's people.

We need in our own time to go to the book of Revelation and read what was said to the church in Laodicea. We need to think about this in the context of Christians plunging into the whole monolithic wave of divorce thinking that it doesn't matter. All they want is to grab another piece of happiness and fulfillment now, to add to their eternal life. There are things that should hit each of us in some area of our lives in reading this.

"These are the words of the Amen, the faithful and true witness, the ruler of God's creation. I know your deeds, that you are neither cold nor hot. I wish you were either one or the other! So because you are lukewarm—neither hot nor cold—I am about to spit you out of my mouth. You say, 'I am rich; I have acquired wealth and do not need a thing.' But you do not realize that you are wretched, pitiful, poor, blind and naked. I counsel you to buy from me gold refined in fire, so you can become rich; and white clothes to wear, so you can cover your shameful nakedness; and salve to put on your eyes, so you can see. Those whom I love I rebuke and discipline. So be earnest, and repent. Here I am! I stand at the door and knock. If anyone hears my voice and opens the door, I will go in and eat with him, and he with me. To him that overcomes, I will give the right to sit with me on my throne, just as I sat down with my Father on his throne. He who has an ear to hear, let him hear what the Spirit says to the churches." (Revelation 3:14-22)

How many of us are concerned about whether or not we are overcoming in the battle with Satan? How many of us long to be refined even though it is in fire? How many of us want to have salve on our eyes so we can see? The call to repent is quickly followed by the reminder that our Shepherd, our Lord, is knocking at the door and wants to come in to eat with us. These are words to those of us who have already claimed to believe. We are called to see how very blind we are in danger of becoming, as the church today accepts the opposite of what God's Word teaches as all right.

Have you read what God said in Malachi? It may be frightening to read, but we aren't supposed to avoid the strong words of warning.

Another thing you do: You flood the Lord's altar with tears. You weep and wail because he no longer pays attention to your offerings or accepts them with pleasure from your hands. You ask, "Why?" It is because the Lord is acting as the witness between you and the wife of your youth, because you have broken faith with her, though she is your partner, the wife of your marriage covenant. Has not the Lord made them one? In flesh and spirit they are his. And why one? Because he was seeking godly offspring. So guard yourself in your spirit, and do not break faith with the wife of your youth. "I hate divorce," says the Lord God of Israel, "and I hate a man's covering himself with violence as well as with his garment," says the Lord Almighty. So guard yourself in your spirit, and do not break faith. You have wearied your Lord with your words. "How have we wearied Him?" you ask. By saying, "All who do evil are good in the eyes of the Lord, and he is pleased with them" or "Where is the God of justice?" (Malachi 2:13-17)

The picture given here is a very clear one. Youthful marriages are meant to continue to old age, or to the time of the death of one of the two. Continuity is meant to be worked upon. A relationship takes time and work, putting oneself last, rather than clamoring for rights and happiness all the time. Christians' marriages are meant to be an allegory of the relationship of God and His people, a relationship of love. Love suffers long and is kind. Theirs should be a long-suffering that is really worked at, with determination to have continuity in spite of the world's atmosphere and the weaknesses and faults of each of the two people. In a finite and limited way, just as the word *father* should mean someone filled with tenderness, compassion, strength, and protection as well as someone who can give good counsel and help, so the word *husband* is meant to carry with it qualities which remind one of Christ the Bridegroom. What a counterfeit picture is being given and what a robbery has taken place, a robbery of the meaning of such words as *faithfulness, trustworthiness, dependability, service*. How can any of us learn to serve God if we never are willing to pay a price of discomfort in any way to serve another human being?

Just as many people become Christians for what they "can get out of it," what they can get from God in a relationship with Him, rather than what they can do for Him and how they can show Him thankfulness and love in some practical way, so many people get married thinking of what they can "get out of it" in sexual fulfillment, in being happy! When things don't go well and troubles come, no base has been prepared in either the relationship with the Lord or with the husband or wife to put self last and to use the very opportunity of the rough or dark time to make something really creative out of the relationship. Imagination is needed in the days when the job is lost, a fire destroys the garage, there is a car accident, the child you are waiting for has not come home from school but is in the hospital, the taxes are unfairly high, the priceless heirloom was dropped and broken. Imagination is needed to recognize just what "for better or for worse" is all about, and to have some pride in working at it.

First Corinthians 6:12-19 talks to the Corinthians about the sexual immorality of that time, which was similar to ours. Paul says the body is not for sexual immorality, but for the Lord. Then he goes on to speak of the resurrection of Christ's body and ours also. In other words the body is not bad, is not unimportant, but is so precious that Christ died so that our bodies will be raised from the dead. With this as a background, then comes the admonition to not go to prostitutes. Verse 16 makes clear the reason: "Do you not know that he who unites himself with a prostitute is one with her in body? For it is said, 'The two will become one flesh.' But he who unites himself with the Lord is one with him in spirit."

What a terrific comparison!

There is a mystical oneness God has made possible in the sexual relationship which belongs not to promiscuousness, but to a continuity in marriage, because it parallels the eternal oneness we have when we are united with the Lord. Once we belong to the Lord it is forever. It is not a casual relationship, and Christians are meant to realize that their precious bodies which will be raised from the dead one day are to have their sexual relationships in the right framework. To make sex the integration point in life, and to seek fulfillment in any way that comes into one's mind or onto one's path is taking that which has been created for one purpose and using it for a very different thing.

Have you ever seen the loving care with which a maker of fine wood furniture gathers wood and seasons it, preparing it for just the right matching of grain in making his chairs and cabinets and tables? Think of someone wanting to warm himself in front of a fire coming and chopping up all that precious oak, walnut, cherry, mahogany, and making a fire in the fireplace as he sits and eats and drinks by the blaze. What a waste!

No illustrations are perfect, but sex, which is a central factor in manipulating human beings today, and a central factor in breaking up marriages in so many parts of the world, is being twisted into that which destroys the Who am I? and the How can I be fulfilled? altogether. It is like the fire made with the valuable and rare wood with its matched grain all ready for something beautiful. It has been misused.

The passage in 1 Corinthians goes on: "Flee from sexual immorality. All other sins a man commits are outside his body, but he who sins sexually sins against his own body. Do you not know that your body is a temple of the Holy Spirit, who is in you, whom you have received from God? You are not your own; you were bought at a price. Therefore honor God with your body."

There are three more reasons for not committing sexual sin: First, it is a sin against your own body which is not made for such use. Second, it is a terrible thing to use your body, which really is lived in by the Holy Spirit, for that which is sinful. Third, you have been bought because Jesus died in your place, so you don't belong to yourself anymore.

There is so very much talk about people owning their own bodies today—especially by women who claim that they have a right not only to do what they want to sexually, but to make their bodies a graveyard for their own children, the relative that is closest to them. For a Christian, all the talk about a "right to my body" is all wrong! Our bodies belong to the One who died so that we can be certain of having transformed bodies that will be perfect for all eternity. They have been paid for by Jesus, and we need to study how we are supposed to use them, and recognize sin and ask forgiveness for what we have done wrong with our bodies.

The seventh chapter of 1 Corinthians goes right on to the next question those men would have asked. "What can we do now? We've blown it! We've already done all those things." It seems to me this would be a portion of what they would be asking. And the answer is in the context of the immorality of that day. The culture of that time was similar to today, and as with the whole Bible, the answer fits our time and needs to be constantly remembered by each of us.

But since there is so much immorality, each man should have his own wife, and each woman her own husband. The husband should fulfill his marital duty to his wife, and likewise the wife to her husband. (7:2)

The *King James Version* says, "to avoid fornication, let every man have his own wife." The whole teaching here is that in addition to the sexual portion of marriage being for oneness, now that the fallen world is so full of the wrong use of sex, so full of immorality in this area of life, the way of keeping away from immorality should be the fulfillment of each person's need within the framework of marriage. Since this is to help people living in a culture which is full of temptations to stay away from them, it follows very definitely that there is meant to be an attempt to care for each other's needs. But note that there is no one-sidedness in what is outlined here; there is a careful admonition which indicates that each one is to care for the other person's needs, rather than only fighting for rights. But the unselfish regard for the other person means that there are no excuses for withdrawal or denial or coldness in the physical area of marriage. It would be as serious if a wife or husband refused to cook or provide a meal because of not feeling hungry, and at the same time refused to talk during the mealtime and eat with the other one because of feeling hostile. Each day requires working at it, even when it does not flow naturally. It must be a growing-together relationship, so that a wall is being built against the invasion of what Satan will try to throw into your marriage to spoil it.

Read on: "The wife's body does not belong to her alone but also to her husband. In the same way, the husband's body does not belong to him alone but also to his wife. Do not deprive each other except by mutual consent and for a time, so that you may devote yourselves to prayer."

This is extremely clear. When you say "I do," you have given your body to each other, according to biblical teaching, and selfishness is out. The only proper reason given for depriving the other one of the physical relationship is that time may be had for prayer. And this special time to be taken for prayer is to be a decision by mutual consent. It is a kind of fasting and prayer which is decided on together for some special reason, even as a meal is put aside to spend that time in prayer for some special reason. It is important in the years of married life to take time for a day of prayer or hours of prayer, when serious decisions are before one. "Should we leave this state and go a thousand miles away to another job, another location?" "Should we go to Africa to teach?" "We need to take time to pray for the children in this situation." "While Jim is traveling, let's agree to pray one hour a day for him." This agreeing to pray together, mutually aware of the need, should be a part of married life that is bringing a spiritual oneness. It is not right, according to this instruction about the physical side of married life in Corinthians, to say, "No, not tonight, I'm going to pray," and then to go off feeling pious about being more spiritual than the other person.

The next sentence makes it very specific that the person turning away and refusing is involved in any fall that may come because of a temptation. The warning is like the blast of a horn in order to capture attention.

Listen: "Then come together again so that Satan will not tempt you because of your lack of self-control."

This is the last half of verse 5, which says that the only reason for staying apart is for prayer. Notice that the time of prayer is not to be counted on to push away the temptation, but that a practical protection is given in order to foil Satan. The word here is that, "To avoid having your children steal buns from the bakery, have fresh baked buns waiting for them at home after school." It is the same kind of practical warning that if marriage is indeed to help people stay away from immorality, then there should be a responsibility taken by each of the two to fulfill each other's needs as much as possible.

Jesus takes the sin of adultery a step further, into the mind, hidden from other people, but not from God. In Matthew 5:27-30 He continues to speak on that hillside where He has just been speaking about murder. Now He says: "You have heard it said, 'Do not commit adultery.' But I tell you that anyone who looks at a woman lustfully has already committed adultery with her in his heart. If your right eye causes you to sin, gouge it out and throw it away. It is better for you to lose one part of your body than for your whole body to be thrown into hell."

This is leading up to His saying, "Be ye perfect as my Father in heaven is perfect." And indeed, we are not going to be perfect until Jesus comes back again to change us; but this is our standard, our goal, that which we need to be aware of and to ask the Lord's help to do. We are not to accept adultery. Inside our own prayer life we even need to be confessing *any* thought that is out of line, and asking Him for forgiveness, let alone any plans to blatantly go ahead with actions that are acceptable to our culture but not to God.

Who makes the rules?

In case any of us is tempted to see everyone else's sin in this area and not our own, Jesus made very plain the need to judge ourselves first. In John 8:6-11 Jesus is speaking after the Pharisees brought him a woman caught in adultery. They asked if He would have them stone her, as the law of Moses had commanded.

> They were using this question as a trap, in order to have a basis for accusing him. But Jesus bent down and started to write on the ground with his finger. When they kept on questioning him, he straightened up and said to them, "If any one of you is without sin, let him be the first to throw a stone at her." Again he stooped down and wrote on the ground. At this, those who heard began to go away one at a time, the older ones first, until only Jesus was left, with the woman still standing there. Jesus straightened up and asked her, "Woman where are they? Has no one condemned you?" "No one, sir," she said. "Then neither do I condemn you," Jesus declared. "Go now and leave your life of sin."

Then as Paul preaches to the Jews in Romans 2, he calls on them to be honest before God, saying, "You who say that people should not commit adultery, do you commit adultery? . . . You who brag about the law, do you dishonor God by breaking the law? As it is written, 'God's name is blasphemed among the Gentiles because of you.' " How searching is God's Word. It does not leave any one of us out. What are we doing that endangers the blaspheming of God's name among the unbelievers?

"But," you may say, "adultery is that sin committed by married people who are unfaithful to their vows. What about me, I'm not married?"

The teaching of the whole Word of God is fair. There has been a fall, the world is not now what God made it to be. There have been, and are, myriads of viruses and germs that bring diseases which were not a part of His perfect creation. There are earthquakes, tornadoes, hurricanes, extreme heat, extreme cold, storms, and disasters of all kinds which spoil the perfection of all that was made. As for human beings, as we have seen, from the time Adam and Eve chose to put Satan's word above God's, there has been a lopsided living, and a constant history throughout centuries of human beings living not on the basis of who they are, but on a variety of false bases. The sin that has affected every human being has spoiled what could have been had it not been in existence. And until all nature is restored and the terrible vandalization of God's creation changed by the return of Christ, the effects of the fall are going to continue to be a part of the life experience of each of us.

Why say all that again?

Because it is impossible to see reality without first seeing how the fall affects everything. No one is perfect physically, psychologically, intellectually, emotionally, or spiritually. Accepting Christ as Savior, becoming one of the sheep of His pasture, being born into the family of the eternal God, entering into a place that is ours among the people of God—this does not bring us perfection in all the areas of our lives. Each blind person accepting the Lord does not suddenly see with his or her physical eyes, each deaf person does not hear, each person with amputated legs and arms does not suddenly grow new legs and arms, each person whose brain was hurt by an accident at birth does not suddenly become able to function perfectly, each person with an organ missing does not suddenly grow a new organ and have proper bowel or digestion functioning. But it is not just people born with physical defects who do not have new bodies the moment they are born into the Lord's family. Christians who get paralyzed in a sudden accident, so that from being healthy athletes one day they are changed to being handicapped, or get cancer or some other disabling disease have to change their life pattern drastically. There is no promise that such things will not hit if you have enough faith. Paul was hit with drastic difficulties, including his thorn in the flesh. And Stephen was hit with stones which knocked the life out of him, in the middle of preaching a marvelous sermon. It is extremely important to rethink all this in connection with sexual fulfillment being a problem to any one of us! Where is the promise that the effects of the fall will be removed immediately from us when we become Christians, so that every desire or even basic need will be completely fulfilled in this life?

Think a moment about talents. We all have hidden possibilities which are never developed, due to time, money, opportunities, hindrances of various sorts. For each of us there are disappointments and frustrations which seem overwhelming at times. The variety of illustrations would be endless. Expectations of marriage being a glorious constant fulfillment are not met, and the realization that the relationship is similar to slogging on in a career of another sort, to bring forth something tangible out of imperfect ingredients, is not easy to accept and go on with.

To take the frustration of not being married, or of not having any inclination toward the other sex at all, or of only feeling inclined sexually toward things that are outside of the framework God has commanded, and to think that this makes a life of conforming to the biblical teaching impossible is to forget the impossible words Jesus spoke to the rich young ruler. In the light of that passage, the possibility of really turning to God and saying, "Everything is yours, and I am turning to you and away from all else," is just as hard for people who need to turn away from one kind of thing that has a central place within their thoughts or emotions as another. Jesus would say to the homosexual and lesbian the same kind of thing as to the opera singer who becomes a missionary and never sings again. "With man it is impossible, but all things are possible to God."

Why must there be a turning away? Why do we not each have a right to demand health, wealth, happiness, and sexual fulfillment in a broken and fallen world once we have become God's people? Why do we not have a right to demand it even if in a framework that is not His, and does not conform to what He made us to be as male and female?

Read two passages together to sit under God's strong words.

Way back in Abraham's time God made it strikingly clear that the annulling of His creation of male and female, whose physical oneness was to be a wonderful picture of spiritual oneness with God, was a horrible sin, a terrible twisting thing that gave a blasphemous caricature of what He had created. In Sodom and Gomorrah, the cities Lot had chosen to live in, there had been a growing turning away from the male-female relationship in sex, and men only desired to have sex with other men. God tells Abraham He is going to wipe out these two cities completely because they are so heinous to Him. They were so abnormal that He wanted no more generations to be brought forth in this place. Abraham pleads for the cities, asking that if there are some who are not sinful but who still worship God, that for the sake of these would God please save those cities. You remember Abraham started with the possibility of fifty, then came to just ten. And there were not even ten people left who were true to the Lord.

God sent two angels, who evidently looked like men, to visit Lot and tell him to take his family out and flee, before the "bomb" hit. This is in Genesis 19. Do you remember that the men of the city, young and old, surrounded the house screaming for the angels to be brought out to them? Verse 5: "They called to Lot, 'Where are the men [angels] who came to you tonight? Bring them out so that we can have sex with them.' " As they tried to break in the door, the angels drew Lot back into the house and supernaturally took care of the situation by striking all the men with blindness.

The destruction of Sodom and Gomorrah was complete. On the shores of the Dead Sea one finds salt wasteland to this day! God has left a reminder in the land, as well as the account in His Word, that sodomy was sinful, is sinful. Sodomy, along with divorce without a proper reason, is a part of the "you shall not" of the seventh commandment.

Come to Romans and read the description of the sinfulness of human beings, spoiled through the ages, and find how today's history is being described. Sin is not less sinful because "everybody does it." A solution for sin is needed, not a lax attitude of getting used to it.

> For although they knew God, they neither glorified him as God nor gave thanks to him, but their thinking became futile and their foolish hearts were darkened. . . . Because of this, God gave them over to shameful lusts. Even their women exchanged natural relations for un-

natural ones. In the same way the men also abandoned natural relations with women and were inflamed with lust for one another. Men
committed indecent acts with other men, and received in themselves
due penalty for their perversion. Furthermore, since they did not
think it worthwhile to retain the knowledge of God, he gave them over
to a depraved mind, to do what ought not to be done. They have
become filled with every kind of wickedness, evil, greed and deprav-
ity. They are full of envy, murder, strife, deceit and malice. They are
gossips, slanderers, God-haters, insolent, arrogant and boastful; they
invent ways of doing evil; they disobey their parents; they are senseless, faithless, heartless, ruthless. Although they know God's righteous
decree that those who do such things deserve death, they not only
continue to do these very things but also approve of those who practice
them. (Romans 1:21, 26-32)

Ouch! What an uncomfortable list. We are all hit.

It is right here that we are conscious of the flow of sin that came
forth from Adam's sin. We are to be forcibly struck with the awe
and wonder of the brilliant shaft of sunlight in the midst of all this
darkness. "For if the many died by the trespass of the one man,
how much more did God's grace and the gift that came by the grace
of the one man, Jesus Christ, overflow to the many" (Romans 5:15).
There *is* hope. There *is* a solution. At any point there is the possibility of turning to the Lord in answer to the cry, "Turn from your
evil ways," and of knowing that there is forgiveness and help to go
on.

First Corinthians 6:9-11 tells very openly what kind of people
had turned to Christ and were right then a part of the church. "Do
you not know that the wicked will not inherit the kingdom of God?
Do not be deceived: Neither the sexually immoral nor idolaters nor
adulterers nor male prostitutes nor homosexual offenders nor
thieves nor the greedy nor drunkards nor slanderers nor swindlers
will inherit the kingdom of God. And that is what some of you
were. But you were washed, you were sanctified, you were justi-
fied in the name of the Lord Jesus Christ and by the Spirit of our
God." It is to these people that Paul is outlining the reality of the
Christian life in the power of the Holy Spirit. It is to these people
Paul is speaking when He says that we are to walk in the light.
There is to be a change.

When there is discussion in churches concerning having homosexual pastors "because times have changed," when there is a tendency to think of no-fault divorce as an acceptable thing among Christians, when there are lesbian marriages taking place in church weddings, when on every side there is an exchange of bitter for sweet and evil for good in all the areas which relate to the seventh commandment—when all this happens, are we going to be embarrassed to do anything at all about it?

Whatever we do, we do not do it as perfect people singling out the imperfect to thunder at. We act as weak people who can do nothing at all without the moment by moment cry, "Give me Thy strength in my weakness, Lord, to go on one more hour," whatever our weakness. Our time is short! There is a measured piece of time ahead for us. We are admonished: "Be on your guard; stand firm in the faith; be men [people] of courage; be strong. Do everything in love" (1 Corinthians 16:13).

The truth of what God made us to be in the first place and what He is preparing for us to enjoy in our new bodies needs to be made known. It must have a practical part in influencing our decisions on a personal basis—and in our voting, our choice of church, our choices of schools, our choices of books and magazines to have in our homes, our choices of towns and cities to live in, as well as our activity in political areas.

The sacrifices we need to make to live in line with the commandments of God must be recognized as an integral part of actively believing that the Lord is really coming back, and that one day we will not only rejoice to be in our new bodies, but will stand at the believer's judgment in our new bodies. And when our child asks us, as in Deuteronomy 6:20, 21, " 'What is the meaning of the stipulations, decrees and laws the Lord our God has commanded you?' tell him . . ."

8: THE EIGHTH COMMANDMENT

Years ago when my daughter Susan and her husband Ranald Macaulay were working in Ealing, London, in the branch of L'Abri which they had commenced there as a place where people came for discussion, for morning-coffee Bible studies, for individual help, as well as for church services on Sunday and lectures Saturday night, they had quite a diverse cross section of people—from the most highly placed people, brilliant scientists or artists or businessmen and women, to some who were on parole from prison. One dear man who had lived a life of the professional thief and found, in his new keen interest, all he was learning about Christianity to be quite fascinating was trying to go straight during this time of parole. He hadn't quite got the hang of it, so to speak!

One night after a church service Ranald was taking this man home to the place where he slept, and they were having quite a good chat about the content of the sermon. Ran felt very pleased with the man's progress in understanding. Suddenly as they rounded a corner, the man looked out of the window of the car and started, "Ooooo blimey, Ranald, look 'ere, look 'ere. Y' know w'at? 'ere's the best place to get into that ever was. See up there? Y'a c'n make it up over that wall and put a f'ot right on that rail. It's an easy one 'at is. Ooooooo, Ranald, c'm on, let's go up. I'll show y'a how. Want to?"

Stealing had been this man's profession, and he had suddenly a surge of warm feeling toward Ranald who had been so kind to him. He wanted to return the kindness with a good tip on how to enter one of the best and easiest places to get a good haul. Right then and there Ranald had a very good opening to explain some details as to what the eighth commandment is all about, and just why it was that the answer was an emphatic, "No, man, no." Why? "You shall not steal" (Exodus 20:15).

Many of us could not relate to that terrific surge of desire to go up the wall and over the windowsill to enter a house as a thief, nor are most of us tempted to become experts at lock-picking, or safe-entering. But the "You shall not steal" is a part of the Ten Commandments which many recognize in their desire to protect their own possessions from thieves. Thus, people agree that there need to be laws—and punishments for breaking them. Yet, the same people are tempted in diverse ways to break that commandment without recognizing or analyzing what is going on.

In the twentieth century it is necessary to establish the fact that individuals, families, groups of people, organizations, and nations are meant to possess material things—lands, houses, food, animals, the results of inventions, talents and the work of people's hands, art works, gold, silver and precious stones. An incredible variety of things are meant to be possessed, to be owned, to belong to one person, or a family, or a company, or an organization, or a nation. If God did not mean people to have a rightful ownership of things, if God did not mean people to be able to earn wages, grow crops, make musical instruments and the fantastic diversity of things that He has enabled human beings to create and to own, then the eighth commandment would not have been given. To say that we are not to steal is to say that things belong to us which someone would want to steal or could steal. Stealing is taking something away from someone to whom it belongs. Therefore, people have a basic right to ownership of certain things.

Who am I? What will fulfill me? God, who made us and knows who we are, has made it very clear that ownership of lands, cattle, wool and flax, and whatever earnings or the work of our hands consists of is a part of who we are. We are made to be creative and to own things which we can be creative with. We are to be fulfilled by industriously using our time to be creative in some way, or a diversity of ways if we have a diversity of talents. If the fall had not spoiled the human beings God had made, the products of creativity would have been far more astonishing than they are. Even in the spoiled and abnormal world which has resulted from the fall, the leftover creativity of human beings brings forth amazing things, from telephones to jets, from tractors to spaceships.

From that point of view, listen to the description of a "wife of noble character," given in Proverbs 31:10-31. I will quote only a few things to illustrate what we are talking about there: "She selects wool and flax and works with eager hands." "She gets up while it is still dark; she provides food for her family and portions for her servant girls." "She sets about her work vigorously; her arms are strong for her tasks." "She considers a field and buys it; out of her earnings she plants a vineyard." "She opens her arms to the poor and extends her hands to the needy."

Forget all else for a moment. This woman, who is held up as an example, possesses wool and flax. She has money that she earned to buy a field and to buy vines to plant. This woman's possessions extend to garments for all her household, and she has enough left over from what she has made to sell. It is because she possesses things that she is able to be compassionate and give out of what she has to the poor. She shares things that belong to her and gives them away willingly. But she could not give what did not belong to her.

God gave Adam and Eve a fantastic estate, the garden of Eden. It was taken away from them when they turned to Satan and believed him rather than God and acted upon that in doing what God had commanded them not to do.

But people were made to be creative with the raw materials God gave them in order to invent, make, design, bring forth, create an overwhelming variety of things. Because of the fall, there have been enormous discrepancies between people as to talents, willingness to work hard, and the kind of discipline that helps an individual to persist in following through a piece of work when others are sitting around doing nothing. These factors have made a great difference in the amount of possessions people have.

Stealing from other people's possessions is one way of trying to even things up! As all the people stood before Moses and he read from that second tablet, they knew the possibilities of stealing. Even though they were in the wilderness, a dry and dusty desert, they owned possessions.

Remember that it was immediately after this that God told Moses to build the tabernacle, so carefully designed by God. People were all to have a part in giving of their possessions and their talents to make that tabernacle a reality. Listen to Exodus 35:20—36:1.

Then the whole Israelite community withdrew from Moses' presence, and everyone who was willing and whose heart moved him came and brought an offering to the Lord for the work on the Tent of Meeting, for all its service, and for the sacred garments. All who were willing, men and women alike, came and brought gold jewelry of all kinds: brooches, earrings, rings and ornaments. They all presented their gold as a wave offering to the Lord. . . . everyone who had acacia wood for any part of the work brought it. Every skilled woman spun with her hands and brought what she had spun—blue, purple, or scarlet yarn or fine linen. And all the women who were willing and had the skill spun the goat hair. The leaders brought onyx stones and other gems to be mounted on the ephod and breastpiece. They also brought spices and olive oil for light and for the anointing oil and for the fragrant incense. All the Israelite men and women who were willing brought to the Lord freewill offerings for all the work the Lord through Moses had commanded them to do.

Then Moses said to the Israelites, "See, the Lord has chosen Bezalel son of Uri, the son of Hur, of the tribe of Judah, and he has filled him with the Spirit of God, with skill, ability and knowledge in all kinds of crafts—to make artistic designs for work in gold, silver and bronze, to cut and set stones, to work in wood and to engage in all kinds of artistic craftsmanship. And he has given both him and Oholiab son of Ahisamach, of the tribe of Dan, the ability to teach others. He has filled them with skill to do all kinds of work as craftsmen, designers, embroiderers in blue, purple, and scarlet yarn and fine linen, and weavers—all of them master craftsmen and designers. So Bezalel, Oholiab and every skilled person to whom the Lord has given skill and ability to know how to carry out all the work of constructing the sanctuary are to do the work just as the Lord has commanded."

We could take a lot of time to speak of the interest of our Creator in giving people artistic talents, as well as His interest in beauty down to the finest details. We could read and reread and discover the art works God commanded to be made. Instead, I'll just recommend my husband's book *Art and the Bible* for a fuller treatment of this important subject. In order to understand this eighth commandment, we must be certain that God meant human beings to have possessions—and to have a diversity of skills and willingness to work to produce more possessions or to earn money to buy more. Not only did the people not all have exactly the same possessions; they did not possess the same skills, nor were they all masters of the crafts. To have some indicated as masters meant others were not as good. We do not know what it would have been like if there had been no fall and people had not been sinful. But as it is now and has been through all history, people are not ever equal in their talents, skills, industriousness, and persistence in work. Nor are they equal in their possession of raw materials. Whether we are talking about nations or individuals, there has always existed the right of possession or ownership, and there has always been the temptation to take what is not one's own. Stealing would be a meaningless word if everything belonged equally to everybody.

Stealing, however, is not the way to become the possessor of possessions!

Habakkuk 2 gives a portion of the Lord's answer to his prophet when he complains about the violence and injustice of that period, which he thinks should be put to a swift end.

> "Woe to him who builds his realm by unjust gain
> to set his nest on high,
> to escape the clutches of ruin!
> You have plotted the ruin of many peoples,
> Shaming your own house and forfeiting your life.
> The stones of the wall will cry out,
> and the beams of the woodwork will echo it."
> (vv. 9-11)

> "Woe to him who piles up stolen goods
> and makes himself wealthy by extortion!"
> (v. 6)

In Micah 6:9-11 God speaks in judgment of what Israel has been doing, after His redeeming them out of Egypt. He tells of not being pleased with offerings made from ill-gotten gains.

Listen! The Lord is calling to the city—
　　and to fear your name is wisdom—
　　"Heed the rod and the One who appointed it.
Am I still to forget, O wicked house,
　　your ill-gotten treasures
　　and the short ephah, which is accursed?
Shall I acquit a man with dishonest scales,
　　with a bag of false weights?"

A similar denouncement is made in Micah 2:1-3.

Woe to those who plan iniquity,
　　to those who plot evil on their beds!
At morning's light they carry it out
　　because it is in their power to do it.
They covet fields and seize them,
　　and houses, and take them.
They defraud a man of his home,
　　a fellowman of his inheritance.
Therefore, the Lord says:
"I am planning disaster against this people,
　　from which you cannot save yourselves.
You will no longer walk proudly,
　　for it will be a time of calamity."

Defrauding people out of their lands or houses, whatever "cover" the business has, is all a part of the blatant disobedience of the commandment not to steal. God is not fooled. There is coming a judgment, no matter how successful stealing seems to be, whether by fraud and violence, by tricky small print people don't notice, or by pressure to foreclose a widow's mortgage.

There are also descriptive warnings given, such as in Amos 5:11-13.

You trample on the poor
　　and force him to give you grain.
Therefore, though you have built stone mansions,
　　you will not live in them;
Though you have planted lush vineyards,
　　you will not drink their wine.
For I know how many are your offenses
　　and how great your sins.

> You oppress the righteous and take bribes
> and you deprive the poor of justice in the courts.
> Therefore the prudent man keeps quiet in such times,
> for the times are evil.
> Seek good, not evil, that you may live.

God makes very specific the command not to steal from the people working for you. The employer is given very strong admonition to be scrupulously fair with his employees. The farmer and vineyard grower is to be fair with his workers. Instructions are explicit.

> "Do not steal. Do not lie. Do not deceive one another. . . . Do not hold back the wages of a hired man overnight." (Leviticus 19:11, 13)

> "Do not take advantage of a hired man who is poor and needy, whether he is a brother Israelite or an alien living in one of your towns. Pay him his wages each day before sunset, because he is poor and is counting on it. Otherwise he may cry to the Lord against you, and you will be guilty of sin." (Deuteronomy 24:14)

The command not to steal carries over into dealing quickly and fairly for anyone working for us. We are to be sensitive to their needs and not make the person with less than we have wait for their payment. To withhold what is due rather than give it immediately is linked with the act of stealing.

The next step is the strong command not to fail to leave something in the fields for someone to glean after the harvest has been gathered in. We will see later what God says about our sharing what we have, giving gifts, and caring for people. This command is something else. It isn't counted among the gifts, it isn't put into statistics. It is an untabulated amount left for anyone to come and take, left in the field for poor people to come and gather for their needs.

> "When you reap the harvest of your land, do not reap to the very edges of your field or gather the gleanings of your harvest. Do not go over your vineyard a second time or pick up the grapes that have fallen. Leave them for the poor and the alien. I am the Lord your God." (Leviticus 19:9, 10)

> When you are harvesting in your field and you overlook a sheaf, do not go back to get it. Leave it for the alien, the fatherless and the widow, so

that the Lord your God may bless you in all the work of your hands. When you beat the olives from your trees, do not go over the branches a second time. Leave what remains for the alien, the fatherless and the widow. When you harvest the grapes in your vineyard, do not go over the vines again. Leave what remains for the alien, the fatherless and the widow. Remember that you were slaves in Egypt. That is why I command you to do this. (Deuteronomy 24:19-22)

You may say, "I don't have a field," and feel that there is no possible application of this gleaning in your life. It seems to me we need to try to translate something of this into all of our lives. For me, leaving something in the corner of the fields, or a few grapes on the vines can be a larger than necessary tip to a weary-looking waitress, or a taxi driver who isn't expecting it, or a man lugging bags on the station platform, one on his shoulder, balancing the others in his hands. It can be for people we don't know and may never see again, who can't thank us personally, and for whom the small gleaning means something even though we can't count it among tax-free receipts! Some very practical way of sharing food, or our catch of fish, or clothing can also be like this. You can use your imagination, and I must use mine, to see how we can leave some sort of grapes or grain in the field to be helpful to strangers. We can add a very silent prayer, asking the Lord to use it in some special way for that individual, as well as telling the Lord we are doing it unto Him too. It is an uncounted portion of the harvest, which is the opposite of scraping up every last bit of it. A generosity ordered by God!

We are not to steal other people's money, possessions, time, or energy. We are to be sensitive to the need not to rob people, to give fair weights and measures in every sense of that idea—in the larger sense, as well as in the sense of a pound of beans containing a full pound.

However, there is an even more serious kind of robbing going on among human beings, especially those who are counted among God's people. In Israel's time it was made very clear that a portion of everything was to be given to the Lord. In Genesis 14:18-20 we have the mention of Abraham giving a tenth of everything.

Then Melchizedek king of Salem [that is, Jerusalem] brought out bread and wine. He was priest of the God Most High, and he blessed Abram, saying,

"Blessed be Abram by God Most High,
  Creator of heaven and earth.
And blessed be God Most High,
  who delivered your enemies into your hand."

Then Abram gave him a tenth of everything.

This was Abraham's portion given to the Lord, given to the priest of the Lord. Throughout the Old Testament a tithe, or a tenth of what the Lord's people had harvested or had among their flocks or of the things they made with their skill in crafts and arts, was given to the Lord. It was the portion which belonged to the Lord, and to not give it was a very real robbery, made clear by the teaching they all had.

In Deuteronomy 18:1-8, after the twelve tribes had settled in the land, and the tribe of Levi had been chosen by the Lord to be the priestly tribe, caring for the tabernacle and all the things that pertained to worship and the sacrifices, it was made clear that the Levites were to be cared for by the tenth portion of all that the other tribes grew or harvested or made in their professions.

The priests, who are Levites—indeed the whole tribe of Levi—are to have no allotment or inheritance with Israel. They shall live on the offerings made to the Lord by fire, for that is their inheritance. They shall have no inheritance among their brothers; the Lord is their inheritance, as he promised them. This is the share due the priests from the people who sacrifice a bull or a sheep: the shoulder, the jowls, and the inner parts. You are to give them the firstfruits of your grain, new wine and oil, and the first wool from the shearing of your sheep, for the Lord your God has chosen them and their descendants out of all your tribes to stand and minister in the Lord's name always.

In Deuteronomy 26:9-13 we see that this gift to the Lord of the firstfruits, and the tithe, is also to be shared with any who are in need. People are to have help from the portion which is given to the Lord. It has a double use.

"He brought us to this place and gave us this land, a land flowing with milk and honey; and now I bring the firstfruits of the soil that you, O Lord, have given me." Place the basket before the Lord your God and bow down before him. And you and the Levites and the aliens among you shall rejoice in all the good things the Lord your God has given to you and your household. When you have finished setting aside a tenth of all your produce in the third year, the year of the tithe, you shall give it to the Levite, the alien, the fatherless and the widow, so that they may eat in your towns and be satisfied.

Is it possible to steal from God?

What an idea—that a finite, weak, sinful human being could steal from the all-powerful Creator who is the Almighty God! Yet we are told that we are in danger of robbing God. We need to find out how that can be.

Do the horrible headlines of today's papers matter to the living God? Does He notice when cruelty of person to person makes thousands of people into refugees? Does He see into the refugee camps where refugees are stealing food from other refugees and are black-marketing, exchanging their own children's food for cigarettes and other things? Does such extreme wickedness, which so disappoints the people who have gone halfway around the world to help and bring aid, also disappoint God, who for so many centuries has come to give aid to generation after generation of people only to be rejected? Robbing and misusing supplies which have been given with great compassion is a crushing disillusionment for many who have given time and energy to help.

But what about God?

"So I will come near to you for judgment. I will be quick to testify against sorcerers, adulterers and perjurers, against those who defraud laborers of their wages, who oppress the widows and the fatherless, and deprive aliens of justice, but do not fear me," says the Lord Almighty.

"I, the Lord, do not change. So you, O descendants of Jacob, are not destroyed. Ever since the time of your forefathers you have turned away from my decrees and have not kept them. Return to me, and I will return to you," says the Lord Almighty.

"But you ask, 'How are we to return?'

"Will a man rob God? Yet you rob me.

"But you ask, 'How do we rob you?'

"In tithes and offerings. You are under a curse—the whole nation of you—because you are robbing me. Bring the whole tithe into the storehouse, that there may be food in my house. Test me in this," says the Lord Almighty, "and see if I will not throw open the floodgates of heaven and pour out so much blessing that you will not have room enough for it. I will prevent pests from devouring your crops, and the vines in your fields will not cast their fruit," says the Lord Almighty. "Then all the nations will call you blessed, for yours will be a delightful land," says the Lord Almighty.

"You have said harsh things against me," says the Lord. "Yet you ask, 'What have we said against you?'

"You have said, 'It is futile to serve God. What did we gain by carrying out his requirements and going about like mourners before the Lord Almighty? But now we call the arrogant blessed. Certainly the evildoers prosper, and even those who challenge God escape.' " (Malachi 3:5-14)

How very much like people today! People now say exactly the same thing. "What difference does it make to serve the Lord? The wicked ones seem to prosper a lot more. Why bother! Nothing will happen to us if we turn our backs and just work for success, material gain, and power. God isn't doing anything." But Malachi goes on to tell what God replies to all this.

Then those who feared the Lord talked with each other, and the Lord listened and heard. A scroll of remembrance was written in his presence concerning those who feared the Lord and honored his name.

"They will be mine," says the Lord Almighty, "in the day when I make up my treasured possession. I will spare them, just as in compassion a man spares his son who serves him. And you will again see the distinction between the righteous and the wicked, between those who serve God and those who do not." (Malachi 3:16-18)

Take heart! Courage! The Lord is noticing when we talk about Him, as well as when we talk directly to Him. He is "taking notes"; "a scroll of remembrance" is being written. The difference it makes to be serving Him and asking for help to serve Him better is all the difference in the world! The difference it makes when we discover that we cannot keep the law by ourselves, but that Christ has kept it for us, as well as dying for us is all the difference! The difference it makes having the Holy Spirit within us to help us moment by moment in the midst of the battle is all the difference! Indeed, one day "you will see the distinction . . . between those who serve God and those who do not."

Is it only in the Old Testament that giving proportionately of one's material possessions to God is spoken of? Is it still possible to be considered by God as robbing Him? Is this commandment to not steal no longer important? Or is it more important than ever to be both honest in our dealings with other people and honest in our giving to God? Since we are not "under the law, but under grace," does that mean we may steal?

Read Ephesians 4:25, 28.

> Therefore each of you must put off falsehood and speak truthfully to his neighbor, for we are all members of one body. . . . He who has been stealing must steal no longer, but must work doing something useful with his own hands, that he may have something to share with those in need.

This defines something of what it means to put off old attitudes and to be made new in the attitudes of your minds. It is practical, and it does not deny God's unchangeable law. It is simply a matter of understanding how we can be forgiven when we need to be forgiven, as well as understanding what our sin is. Then we have help in having a growing change take place.

How amazing that the work which is now to take the place of stealing is to bring a gain to the man or woman working, enough to care for his or her own needs as well as enough to be shared. Possessions are still going to be a part of the Christian's life. To share indicates that there is to be something to share.

> Now about the collection for God's people: Do what I told the Galatian churches to do. On the first day of every week, each one of you should set aside a sum of money in keeping with his income, saving it up, so that when I come no collections will have to be made. (1 Corinthians 16:1, 2)

Each person was to give proportionately, and the income differed!

In 2 Corinthians 8:2-7 Paul tells the Corinthian church about the selfless giving of the Macedonian churches, which evidently were made up of poor people.

> Out of the most severe trial, their overflowing joy and their extreme poverty welled up in rich generosity. For I testify that they gave as much as they were able, and even beyond their ability. Entirely on their own, they urgently pleaded with us for the privilege of sharing in this service to the saints. And they did not do as we expected, but they gave themselves first to the Lord and then to us in keeping with God's will. . . . But just as you excel in everything—in faith, in speech, in

knowledge, in complete earnestness and in your love for us—see that you also excel in this grace of giving.

Paul is urging the Corinthian church to consider giving as very important in the midst of the other basic things he lists. He goes on in greater detail in chapter 9, commending them on their giving and urging them to continue.

> I know your eagerness to help, and I have been boasting about it to the Macedonians, telling them that since last year you in Achaia were ready to give; and your enthusiasm has stirred most of them into action. But I am sending the brothers in order that our boasting about you in this matter should not prove hollow, but that you may be ready, as I said you would be. For if any Macedonians come with me and find you unprepared, we—not to say anything about you—would be ashamed of having been so confident. So I thought it necessary to urge the brothers to visit you in advance and finish the arrangements for the generous gift you had promised. Then it will be ready as a generous gift, not as one grudgingly given. Remember this: Whoever sows sparingly will also reap sparingly, and whoever sows generously will also reap generously. Each man should give what he has decided in his heart to give, not reluctantly or under compulsion, for God loves a cheerful giver. And God is able to make all grace abound to you, so that in all things at all times, having all that you need, you will abound in every good work. As it is written:
>
> "He has scattered abroad his gifts to the poor;
>   his righteousness endures forever."
>
> Now he who supplies seed to the sower and bread for food will also supply and increase your store of seed and will enlarge the harvest of your righteousness. You will be rich in every way so that you can be generous on every occasion, and through us your generosity will result in thanksgiving to God. This service that you perform is not only supplying the needs of God's people but is also overflowing in many expressions of thanks to God. Because of the service by which you have proved yourselves, men will praise God for the obedience that accompanies your confession of the gospel of Christ, and for your generosity in sharing with them and with everyone else. And in their prayers for you their hearts will go out to you, because of the surpassing grace God has given you. Thanks be to God for his indescribable gift! (2 Corinthians 9:1-15)

What overwhelming emphasis on giving!

This does not sound as if the Malachi passage refers only to Old Testament times. If withholding a tenth when God had set that as the amount to give to Him, which went to the people who cared for the tabernacle worship and to the poor also, was called robbing God, how much more we need to search our own attitudes and actions to discover if we are guilty of robbing God now, since God has already given His "indescribable gift" of eternal life through the death of Christ. Our giving is not to be under compulsion. It is to be willingly and cheerfully with love for the Lord and thanksgiving for what He has given us in every way and compassion for the poor we are sharing our material goods with.

Stealing or robbing in our own day can take various forms: not giving a full day's work for a full day's pay, not fulfilling our responsibilities in our daily work, not paying sufficient salaries, or not caring for those who work for us in a human way. We can also be robbing God by not giving generously as we have been urged to do. But notice, no one else is to be the one to tell us what to do. It is according to how God has prospered, and it is to be what we have "decided in the heart to give." It is God who reads our hearts and knows whether we have kept our promises to Him.

Those Macedonians gave out of their poverty. They shared with people who had less than they did and also with the expenses of the apostles. Not everyone, however, was poor and not everyone was told to become poor. Not robbing or stealing, whether from other human beings or God, does not mean it is necessary to have nothing, or even to have very little.

In 1 Timothy 6:6, Paul is telling Timothy what to tell the rich people to do, and of course that extends down through the generations until this present day and until Jesus returns.

> Command those who are rich in this present world not to be arrogant nor to put their hope in wealth, which is so uncertain, but to put their hope in God, who richly provides us with everything for our enjoyment. Command them to do good, to be rich in good deeds, and to be generous and willing to share. In this way they will lay up treasure for themselves as a firm foundation for the coming age, so that they may take hold of the life that is truly life. (1 Timothy 6:17-19)

How special that God made it known to us that we are to have enjoyment in the provisions He makes for us, enjoyment with the things He gives us. We are to enjoy the trees and grass, if He has surrounded us with these, to enjoy the waves of the sea, if that is our view, to enjoy the stars we can see from our tent, or the sunrise we can see from our rowboat. We do not need to feel guilty that everyone cannot have the same thing. But we should recognize and thank God for what He has given us, and then be sure we are carefully giving to Him and sharing what we have to share. To share with others does not cancel out the enjoyment we are meant to have in the midst of our own immediate situation, be it little or much.

It is true that there is an extremely strong warning to rich oppressors, and no Christian should number among the rich oppressors. But that does not condemn all rich people, nor say that no spiritual Christian should be rich. The command is that they should do good, be generous, and be willing to share. Paul has made that clear to Timothy, and to us, as God inspired him in what to say.

James 5:1-6 slashes out against those who would beat down the workers under them for their own gain:

> Now listen, you rich people, weep and wail because of the misery that is coming upon you. Your wealth has rotted, and moths have eaten your clothes. Your gold and silver are corroded. Their corrosion will testify against you and eat your flesh like fire. You have hoarded wealth in the last days. Look! The wages you failed to pay the workmen who mowed your fields are crying out against you. The cries of the harvesters have reached the ears of the Lord Almighty. You have lived on earth in luxury and self-indulgence. You have fattened yourselves in the day of slaughter. You have condemned and murdered innocent men who were not opposing you.

That is the picture of condemnation to those who rob others of their time, energy, talents, and very lives in order to become rich, rather than treating people as human beings with value like their own. However, that is a different thing from saying that prosperity in itself is wrong. From all the history we are given in the Bible we have both the poor and those who have been blessed with good crops and good success described to us as living among the people of God. There is a definite possibility of sharing what we do have, no matter what our circumstances are.

God's infinite wisdom in His marvelous way of enabling us all to do what we can in our own situation, be it hospital bed or the athletic training camp, a street sweeper's job, or Wall Street's high finance, is astounding in its fairness. Yet how he is able to "bank" all that is given is beyond our understanding. It is all hinted at, but is beyond us to understand perfectly until we are shown someday what the richness He has stored up for us is all about, and just what it consists of.

Because, you see, God does not rob anyone. God is perfectly holy, and His character is perfection. He takes what we give directly to Him, what we give to people needing food or shoes or a vacation or a place to live, or to a young person needing an education, or to someone needing to go to a dentist or a doctor—He takes all that and, at the same time, invests it for us. He takes what we give in other ways to our church or to a mission work, to care for the physically hungry or spiritually hungry, and even as it is used to accomplish that task, He invests it for us. He takes our tithe, and all we give above our tithe, and He uses it in three ways at once. He uses it for the immediate thing we gave it for, He accepts it as unto Himself ("when I was hungry you fed me"), and He puts it in that mysterious fund which He has called "treasures in heaven" which we will one day find.

Unfair? Is it unfair that the rich people will have an opportunity always to give more, and the poor always to give less? Unfair? Does it mean we can never catch up and that the ones who have more can always be putting larger amounts in that mysterious treasury? A tithe of a huge amount is so much more than a tithe of a tiny amount. How can it be fair? How can we show our love to the Lord and our appreciation to Him if we are poor in material things, weak physically, or in a wheelchair and a hospital and cannot do the things that come into our minds to do for Him?

First look at Mark 12:41-44.

Jesus sat down opposite the place where the offerings were put and watched the crowd putting their money into the treasury. Many rich people threw in large amounts. But a poor widow came and put in two very small copper coins, worth only a fraction of a penny. Calling his disciples to him, Jesus said, "I tell you the truth, this poor widow has put more money into the treasury than all the others. They all gave out of their wealth; but she, out of her poverty, put in everything—all she had to live on."

The arithmetic is done quite differently! The utter fairness of God's accounts will be astonishing to us all, I am sure. The proportionate giving will make a proportionate treasure in heaven. The Lord will multiply the results some special way beyond anything we are aware of, or so it seems to me. The manner in which Jesus multiplied the gift of the little boy, who gave his whole lunch, and made it into enough lunch for all the thousands of people on that hillside gives us a hint, just a hint of what is being told us.

The same thing is true of love, trust, worship, and adoration of the Lord in the area of winning battles in the war that is going on in the heavenlies. No one is shut out from expressing trust in the most adverse of situations, in depths of despair, in utter exhaustion, in deep sorrow, in great pain, in terrible disappointment, in a wreck by the side of the road, or in a hospital bed. It is sufficient to whisper, "I can't understand, but I still love you, Lord, and I trust you." What has taken place is a victory in the battle between Satan and God as Satan tries to rob God of our love, to rob God of our trust, to steal our attention and fix it on our trouble rather than on God's faithfulness to His promises.

We are so clearly told that God has a treasure for us that cannot be stolen. He has put in a safe place all that we have given Him. "You can't take it with you" is not true when seen in this word of explanation for our daily living now.

> "Do not store up for yourselves treasures on earth, where moth and rust destroy, and where thieves break in and steal. But store up for yourselves treasures in heaven, where moth and rust do not destroy, and where thieves do not break in and steal. For where your treasure is, there your heart will be also." (Matthew 6:19, 20)

Then in Luke, Jesus has just been telling his disciples not to worry about the practical things of life, the food, clothing, and shelter. And He continues in Luke 12:31-34:

> "But seek his kingdom, and these things will be given to you as well. Do not be afraid, little flock, for your Father has been pleased to give you the kingdom. Sell your possessions and give to the poor. Provide

purses for yourselves that will not wear out, a treasure in heaven that will not be exhausted, where no thief comes near and no moth destroys. For where your treasure is, there your heart will be also."

In Hebrews 11 we are told of many of the people who lived by faith, and to whom great promises had been made, but who in their lifetime only saw these promises from afar, with the fulfillment still in the future. We are also given a list of those who suffered terrible afflictions, yet who also were the people of God. Did God rob all these? Has He been robbing us because we expected more *now*? We are given a clear and strong answer, it seems to me, in verses 39 and 40, and then verse 16.

These were all commended for their faith, yet none of them received what had been promised. God had planned something better for us so that only together with us would they be made perfect. (vv. 39, 40)

The day is coming when we will be—with all these who have gone before in the midst of their terrific hardships and afflictions—given new bodies, like Christ's glorious body, in which we can really respond to all the glory which would be too much for us now.

Has God robbed us of anything that is due us as His children? No, a million times no. He is able to say with all the force and integrity of the Creator of the universe, the all-wise and perfect God, the loving and compassionate Heavenly Father:

They were longing for a better country—a heavenly one. Therefore God is not ashamed to be called their God, for he has prepared a city for them. (v. 16)

In the light of all this, surely we should not rob God or people!

9: THE NINTH COMMANDMENT

If the Ten Commandments were a set of pickup sticks to be played in our day-by-day lives, it would be very difficult for anyone to concentrate on picking up one stick without disturbing several others! Picture them lying on a shiny wood table, overlapping each other. We've been picking up the one which said do not steal or do not rob, but already we have moved another stick which had a lot of its weight on this one. It definitely moved! So someone else has a turn to pick up the next one, trying not to touch anything else.

How can you pick up the next commandment without touching or moving any other? It is:

"You shall not give false testimony against your neighbor." (Exodus 20:16)

This is so close to stealing—stealing your neighbor's reputation, stealing your neighbor's chance of getting the new job, stealing your neighbor's sleep at night, putting such worry and despondency upon that neighbor that the weight of slander or false testimony ends in the stealing of that neighbor's life! Already two commandments have been equally involved. Then "you shall not kill" becomes a part of the number of sticks moved when the false testimony begins and the result is suicide. So often even in our finiteness we can see that when one commandment is pulled out to be broken, others have been touched too—not only figuratively, but literally.

Some time ago I read a sad article in a small-town newspaper about a man who had been a good father and husband, an honest man in his profession. He had been unfairly attacked by a newspaper editor who had recently come to town from a distant state, and in an attempted reform had written a number of articles making false insinuations which put blots on this man's reputation. Even though these insinuations were shown to be totally without proof, daily losses of friends' and business associates' trust brought worry, sorrow, and increased frustration. Then came sleepless nights, loss of appetite, and pacing up and down the rooms of the house. The man became a broken person which even a loving family could not help. He went from one kind of withdrawal to another and finally committed suicide. It was a case of being hounded to death, really, by false testimony in the self-appointed court of a writer's pen! The results of this tragedy continue in the lives of the family.

We all know other true cases of the press or media breaking a man or woman and destroying the lives of families as well as one person. We could all tell stories of international proportions, as well as those which are known only to one country, one state, one city, one small town or country area. We know historic stories of this sort as well as current ones. Throughout history human beings have been robbing other human beings of their peace day and night, their pattern of life and work, their energies and creative incentive, their place in the community, their self-respect. All this has been, and is now, taking place because human beings have turned away from living with each other according to the law God gave in the light of who we are and what will fulfill us. For many, many people life has been made miserable or brought to a swift and abrupt end because of others giving false witness, false testimony, telling changed and falsified "facts," giving twisted reports of past history or of incidents that happened yesterday, in newspapers, magazines, books, or letters to be mimeographed and passed around.

The written or printed page is not the only medium for false witness, falsified testimony, exaggerated reports. Today there is also radio, television, and widely publicized hearings or trials spreading far and wide untrue details which may be proven false, but remain in their original false form in the memories of all who saw or heard and formed their own opinions. The effect upon the individuals attacked in this way—as well as their families and their work—is irreparable. It is one of the worst kinds of suffering that can be experienced.

The last six commandments are summed up by "love your neighbor as yourself." This is a positive statement about how to obey each one of the six. Anyone really working at the practical demonstration day by day of love for neighbors would no more plan a campaign of false testimony against anyone else than against himself or herself. The cruelty of person to person is what hits us as we study the commandments. God revealed how to live with fulfillment and peace, but each of us has fallen into the trap of doing the exact opposite and putting self first—and second!

Not only is sin separating people from God as they live in the ugly "freedom" of breaking His commandments. It is also separating them from other human beings and bringing the violence upon their own heads. When the commandment not to give false testimony against a neighbor was given, a very appropriate and strong punishment was also commanded in order to carry out this law. Come to the Bible and read:

> One witness is not enough to convict a man accused of any crime or offense he may have committed. A matter must be established by the testimony of two or three witnesses. If a malicious witness takes the stand to accuse a man of a crime, the two men involved in the dispute must stand in the presence of the Lord before the priests and the judges who are in office at the time. The judges must make a thorough investigation, and if the witness proves to be a liar, giving false testimony against his brother, then do to him as he intended to do to his brother. You must purge this evil from among you. The rest of the people will hear of this and be afraid, and never again will such an evil thing be done among you. Show no pity: life for life, eye for eye, tooth for tooth, hand for hand, foot for foot. (Deuteronomy 19:15-21)

God speaks clearly of the evil, the wickedness of falsely accusing another person, of giving untrue testimony on the stand in court, of lying or twisting and exaggerating so-called "facts" into misrepresenting the truth. It is when such a malicious witness is trying to get someone punished for something he or she did not do that the fiercely drastic "turning the tables" is to take place. The false witness was quite willing to have the other person's eye put out, without any crime having been done, on the basis of his lie. Now the punishment is to fit that crime.

We live in a day, during this last period of the twentieth century, of a wave of increased pressures to give false witness or false testimony. In fact, falsifying facts for gain has become a profession of its own! Think of the ambulance-chasing of some unscrupulous lawyers, offering to split profits if someone testifies to what he or she has "seen," with the facts twisted so that large amounts of money can be collected from an individual or an insurance company. Think of the rapidly mounting instances of malpractice suits where facts are falsified to gain large amounts of money quite unfairly while spoiling the reputation of a careful doctor. Then there are those false witnesses who fill forms and sign papers to say something is wrong, when it is not, in order to sue companies of negligence. A huge money-making business is being built on the base of setting out to break the ninth commandment as often and as cleverly as possible. Fires are rigged up to burn buildings and cars sent over the cliffs in order to claim insurance. Those who break the ninth commandment in this way are every bit as committed to a life of crime as the safe-breaker and other varieties of professional thieves and bandits. There are so many ways to get money by having people give false testimonies that we stumble over new ones day by day. Saying "everybody does it" turns morality into a majority vote rather than the absolute law given by God. We need to use this ninth commandment as a measuring stick to see where we may be tempted to simply shrug our shoulders and ride with the tide with an attitude of, "What does it matter, we can't do anything about it anyway!"

A great deal of false testimony has come into the divorce courts. The film *Kramer versus Kramer* shows quite vividly how lawyers egg on one party against another by exaggerating complaints into the place of false testimonies. Added to the other things involved in divorce—the breaking up of continuity, the breaking up of the oneness of grandparents and parents so that stability is gone for the next generations—comes the terrible private and public breaking of the ninth commandment in turning and twisting facts into false witness. This is done not only by the people involved, but by the lawyers eager to get the fees and the reputation of winning.

Men in politics need to be extremely careful, if indeed they care to be living in the light of the Word of God and in accordance with His commandments, to check and recheck the accuracy of what they say in their speeches so that no false witness is being given. But politics comes into many kinds of organizations, whether it is athletic organizations talking about players or coaches, or business organizations in which one man or woman might be trying to gain leadership by stepping on another, or Christian organizations in which the desire to hold office or gain a place of greater leadership gives rise to cutting down someone else with slightly "off" or untrue remarks. Even in the church from earliest times there has been politicking—pushing someone aside, or annulling the talents or work of someone in the way, or grabbing someone else's rightful place. All this has too frequently been visible to those who have been watching. It is one of the things that causes the world to remark that Christians aren't any different.

Among children in a family or in nursery school, as well as all through educational institutions, one child will tell something that gets another one in trouble, stretching the truth even just a fraction, so one gets ahead by a false witness. Ever since the fall people have been putting each other in a bad light in order to shine by contrast. It is one of the ways the fall affected the actions of human beings. However, not only is it unacceptable to God; it is one of the central kinds of sinful behavior, living on the opposite base from God's law, which makes life unbearable for a majority of people.

Authoritarian governments make false witnesses out of as many people as they can in order to keep the hold on the people, to stamp out individuality, and to enhance mass obedience. Torture has been used, not only in the Spanish Inquisition, but in present-day governments in various parts of the world, to force false testimonies from the lips of people who can bear no more pain and will say anything to put an end to the cruel treatment, not only of themselves, but especially of their children or other members of their families. You and I could easily give examples of this kind from recent news reports.

In another way perhaps, but just as cruelly, authoritarian religious groups force their people to give false witness to things that are not true and have not happened. It is a fearful thing to attach the name of God to things that have never happened, and to use these false testimonies to gain a hearing among unsuspecting people who think they are hearing historic fact. False promises and hopes are often attached in such circumstances to the false testimonies.

> There are six things the Lord hates,
>   seven that are detestable to him:
>   haughty eyes,
>   a lying tongue,
>   hands that shed innocent blood,
>   a heart that devises wicked schemes,
>   feet that are quick to rush into evil,
>   a false witness who pours out lies
>   and a man who stirs up dissension among brothers.
>   (Proverbs 6:16-19)

It is important to memorize what the Lord hates! It is also important to find that hands that shed innocent blood (who is more innocent than an unborn baby and a newly born handicapped baby?) and a heart that devises wicked schemes are directly connected. As the haughty-eyed person with a lying tongue willing to witness to false reports comes into your church, your assembly, your mission station, your hospital staff, your business associates, your political group, your teaching staff, your student association, your farmers association and starts a whispering campaign with some false stories about people, he or she becomes an outstanding one in "stirring up dissension among brothers." It is not hard to stir up dissension!

What is the exact opposite of all this? What is the alternative? What is it the Lord loves and wants us to be and do?

Come now to Matthew 5:7-12 and sit down on the hillside at Jesus' feet. Shut your eyes as you go over what He has said, and think of the contrast, the total difference of this list, and of how hard it is to live up to it.

> "Blessed are the merciful,
>   for they will be shown mercy.
> Blessed are the pure in heart,
>   for they will see God.
> Blessed are the peacemakers,
>   for they will be called the sons of God.
> Blessed are those who are persecuted because of righteousness,
>   for theirs is the kingdom of heaven.

> Blessed are you when people insult you, persecute you and falsely say all kinds of evil against you because of me. Rejoice and be glad, because great is your reward in heaven, for in the same way they persecuted the prophets who were before you."

Two things stand out in this list: *First,* we need the help of the Holy Spirit moment by moment to stay out of the ranks of the false witnesses, to be peacemakers and merciful in our relationship with other people. *Second,* we have joined the ranks of the prophets who have gone before us if we are being spoken against falsely because of our different standards, our different principles, our righteousness, which is that given us by the Holy Spirit, when we stand for very different principles in our school, business, hospital, political life, scientific career, teaching of history or literature. We are to remember that we are in a stream of those who were true to the teaching of the Lord and that there is a special reward for just this kind of affliction. It is not being ignored by the Lord!

David cried out to the Lord in the middle of such an attack in Psalm 27:11, 12—

> Teach me your way, O Lord;
>   lead me in a straight path
>   because of my oppressors.
> Do not turn me over to the desire of my foes,
>   for false witnesses rise up against me,
>   breathing out violence.

It is in the context of this prayer that David goes on to take courage, declaring that he is confident that he will see the goodness of the Lord in the land of the living. So he calls upon us to

"wait for the Lord; be strong and take heart and wait for the Lord."
Many before us have been attacked by false witnesses. We, with
them, need to pray for help, and then to wait for the Lord in a very
real way.

In 1 Peter we see that the oppression of believers by unbelievers
has kept on and will keep on. Our lives are to be lived in contrast to
the world. We should not expect, however, praise and commenda-
tion, but often false accusations.

> Live such good lives among the pagans that, though they accuse you of
> doing wrong, they may see your good deeds and glorify God on the day
> he visits us. (1 Peter 2:12)

Then in 1 Peter 3:13-16—

> Who is going to harm you if you are eager to do good? But even if you
> should suffer for what is right, you are blessed. "Do not fear what they
> fear; do not be frightened." But in your hearts set apart Christ as Lord.
> Always be prepared to give an answer to everyone who asks you to give
> a reason for the hope that you have. But do this with gentleness and
> respect, keeping a clear conscience, so that those who speak malicious-
> ly against your good behavior in Christ may be ashamed of their slan-
> der.

Even though we are going to be slandered and spoken against
falsely, this gives us no excuse to do the same thing. Even though
Christians are "not under law, but under grace," we are not free to
slander and to break the commandment not to give false testimony
against others.

James tells us that the tongue is the most dangerous thing we
have. I would add that any kind of communication could be in-
serted here. Whether we communicate with our tongues, face to
face, whispering in one ear, or loudly over a microphone to hun-
dreds of people in an auditorium, or over the air to millions of
people; whether we write novels or make films—however we communicate, we should recognize that the passage in James is warning us as the people of God that we are to be careful of the possible
results of what we say.

> When we put bits into the mouths of horses to make them obey us, we
> can turn the whole animal. Or take ships as an example. Although they
> are so large and are driven by strong winds, they are steered by a very

small rudder wherever the pilot wants to go. Likewise the tongue is a small part of the body, but it makes great boasts. Consider what a great forest is set on fire by a small spark. The tongue also is a fire, a world of evil among the parts of the body. It corrupts the whole person, sets the whole course of his life on fire, and is itself set on fire by hell. All kinds of animals, birds, reptiles and creatures of the sea are being tamed and have been tamed by man, but no man can tame the tongue. It is a restless evil, full of deadly poison. With the tongue we praise our Lord and Father, and with it we curse men, who have been made in God's likeness. Out of the same mouth come praise and cursing. My brothers, this should not be. Can both fresh water and salt water flow from the same spring? My brothers, can a fig tree bear olives, or a grapevine bear figs? Neither can a salt spring produce fresh water. (James 3:3-12)

Brothers, do not slander one another. Anyone who speaks against his brother or judges him, speaks against the law and judges it. When you judge the law, you are not keeping it, but sitting in judgment on it. There is only one Lawgiver and Judge, the one who is able to save and destroy. But you—who are you to judge your neighbor? (James 4:11, 12)

How often do we pray with the Psalmist, "May the words of my mouth and the meditations of my heart be acceptable to you, O Lord, my God and my Redeemer"? We need to pray for help in this terrific battle against the danger of our own tongues. It is my tongue and your tongue which can kindle a forest fire! We need to pray for help and ask continually that we might not spread a rumor just because we think somebody ought to know. If a report is unnecessary and unkind, and might be just a little exaggerated in our own tongue's rendering of it, and become more exaggerated in the retelling of it the next time, we'd better be silent about it. It is my tongue and your tongue that is likened to a bucking horse that is running away with its rider. It is my tongue and your tongue that is likened to the ship tossing on the waves with the rudder not properly in the hands of the expert. We are called upon as Christians not to slander one another. It is not just that we are to endure false witness against us for the sake of the gospel. It is not just that we are to pray for help when we are falsely slandered. We ourselves are called upon not to "sit in judgment upon the law." We are to sit under the law in each of the Ten Commandments. But in this one we are to remember that we are quite capable of bringing false witness when we fall into judging or when we begin to make brash statements about what we are going to do next year without acknowledging the existence of the Lord's will. To do less than this is called boasting, and that kind of use of the tongue is sin.

The beginning of that passage in James speaks of teachers. If we teach in any way, Sunday school, Bible classes, our neighbors or friends, our own children, we "will be judged more strictly." We must be extremely careful not to imagine we are above this sin or else we will be more tempted by Satan to start one of those forest fires. Satan, who is a liar and the father of lies, wants to get us to slip over the line in any form of false witness or improperly using our tongues.

When the qualifications of elders and deacons are being given along with the admonition that they should be husbands of one wife, the required conversation and carefulness of the wives is also described, in line with James' admonition that teachers will be judged more strictly. "In the same way, their wives are to be women worthy of respect, not malicious talkers but temperate and trustworthy in everything" (1 Timothy 3:11).

In another translation the word deaconesses is substituted for "their wives." So women who are deaconesses, missionaries, Christian workers, teachers, or writers are called upon to be extremely careful about their conversations. They should not be "malicious talkers."

Timothy learned what he knew from his mother and grandmother who had been his teachers and whose faith was commended by Paul. Paul speaks of Timothy having the same faith as these two dear women who had brought him up. So Timothy knew well women who were "temperate and trustworthy in everything," I am sure.

> I thank God, whom I serve, as my forefathers did, with a clear conscience, as night and day I constantly remember you in my prayers. Recalling your tears, I long to see you, so that I may be filled with joy. I have been reminded of your sincere faith, which first lived in your grandmother Lois and in your mother Eunice and, I am persuaded, now lives in you also. (2 Timothy 1:3-5)

The constant reality of living in the world among the enemies of Christ, and poisoning the Lord's people with the slander directed at us by the world, is like a pendulum. We can see ourselves at times like Tarzan, swinging on a long rope over a chasm from a huge tree on one side to another huge tree on the other side. As we try to avoid the chasm by swinging away from the tongues which are slandering us because we are the Lord's people, we swing into the greater danger of slandering others ourselves and breaking that commandment in the safety, so we falsely think, of a Christian circle.

Jeremiah gives us a striking picture of the unbelieving ones. They swing to one side where everyone is against the Lord, as well as His people, and they would be glad to see us fold up like that small-town man being attacked by the editor!

> "They make ready their tongue
>   like a bow, to shoot lies;
> it is not by truth
>   that they triumph in the land.
> They go from one sin to another;
>   they do not acknowledge me," declares the Lord.
> "Beware of your friends;
>   do not trust your brothers.
> For every brother is a deceiver,
>   and every friend is a slanderer.
> Friend deceives friend,
>   and no one speaks the truth.
> They have taught their tongues to lie;
>   they weary themselves with sinning.
> You live in the midst of deception;
>   in their deceit they refuse to acknowledge me,"
>   declares the Lord.
> Therefore this is what the Lord Almighty says:
>   "See, I will refine and test them,
>   for what else can I do
>   because of the sin of my people?
>   Their tongue is a deadly arrow;
>   it speaks with deceit.
>   With his mouth each speaks cordially to his neighbor,
>   but in his heart he sets a trap for him.
>   Should I not punish them for this?"
>   declares the Lord.
>   "Should I not avenge myself
>   on such a nation as this?" (9:3-9)

God hates the cruelty of human beings to human beings. His law has given the only way of living together after the fall without destroying each other. Instead of washing His hands of the human race altogether, God did provide a way to come to Him *now*, a way of living on the basis of the truth and His law, so that in some small way people could learn to treat each other humanly within the framework of who we are and how we can be fulfilled. The only time perfection will be attained and our disappointments come to an end will be when Jesus returns and our changed bodies will never know sin again.

Proverbs sets before us a contrast which is tantalizing. How we long for the tongue that can be described as "choice silver"! If we had less desire for other kinds of success in our lives and more desire for such a gift from the Lord as the kind of conversation that could be called "pure silver," Christians would be different indeed and perhaps the world could see that difference and exclaim loudly, "How they love one another."

> The tongue of the righteous is choice silver,
>   but the heart of the wicked is of little value.
> The lips of the righteous nourish many,
>   but fools die for lack of judgment.
> The blessing of the Lord brings wealth,
>   and he adds no trouble to it.
>   (Proverbs 10:20-22)

In Galatians Paul is speaking of the freedom we have in Christ. We are not under the law now, but are people who have received the Holy Spirit because we have believed what we have heard about Christ, who died for us. We cannot work our way to heaven by trying to obey the law perfectly, because we would fail; we cannot keep it perfectly. Nevertheless, in the midst of all this, Paul speaks strongly of the place of the law in our very living by the Spirit (see Galatians 5:13-23).

> You, my brothers, were called to be free. But do not use your freedom to indulge the sinful nature; rather, serve one another in love. The entire law is summed up in a single command: "Love your neighbor as yourself." If you keep on biting and devouring each other, watch out or you will be destroyed by each other. (vv. 13-15)

What a vivid description of all the diversity of false testimony or false witness which takes place in the Christian circle—the biting and devouring of each other that has taken place in all parts of the earth's geography and in every period of church history! This is one of the sad descriptions of how we as Christians continue to break the ninth commandment. It is not a place where we can say, "Happily we are not under law, so it is all right." It is a place where we are to be brought up short. When did I last "bite and devour" someone in my conversation, with no verbal demonstration of love? Was I sad when someone turned away from the Lord's commands, or did I simply use the occasion to bite and devour with a careless tongue which set a fire? This is the way we need to be checking up on ourselves. Paul goes on to make it even more clear to the Galatians, and to us.

> So I say, live by the Spirit, and you will not gratify the desires of the sinful nature. For the sinful nature desires what is contrary to the Spirit, and the Spirit what is contrary to the sinful nature. They are in conflict with each other, so that you do not do what you want. But if you are led by the Spirit, you are not under law. The acts of the sinful nature are obvious: sexual immorality, impurity and debauchery; idolatry and witchcraft; hatred, discord, jealousy, fits of rage, selfish ambition, dissensions, factions and envy; drunkenness, orgies, and the like. I warn you, as I did before, that those who live like this will not inherit the kingdom of God. But the fruit of the Spirit is love, joy, peace, patience, kindness, goodness, faithfulness, gentleness and self-control. Against such things there is no law. Those who belong to Christ Jesus have crucified the sinful nature with its passions and desires. Since we live by the Spirit, let us keep in step with the Spirit. Let us not become conceited, provoking and envying each other. (vv. 16-23)

This enumeration of the things which demonstrate a Spirit-led walk is not what we see in each other. Too often we see a mixture of the first and second list. Among other of the sins which have been prohibited in the Ten Commandments are "discord" and "dissensions," which would not be if we more carefully asked for help with our tongue. Though a little member, it can sow discord, even as it allows itself to be used to twist and turn a report into a false witness, whether in a formal court or in a whispered conversation.

Galatians does not free us from responsibility; it places more upon us. The solution is to do what we do in the power of the Spirit, asking God for His strength in our weakness.

In 1 Peter 3:10-12 Peter quotes from Psalm 34:12-16—

> "Whoever would love life
>   and see good days
> must keep his tongue from evil
>   and his lips from deceitful speech.
> He must turn from evil and do good;
>   he must seek peace and pursue it.
> For the eyes of the Lord are on the righteous
>   and his ears are attentive to their prayer,
> but the face of the Lord is against those who do evil."

Peter is quoting this in the context of saying that we must live in harmony with one another and be sympathetic, compassionate, and humble. We are not to repay evil with evil or insult with insult, but with blessing. He says that even if we should suffer for doing what is right, we are to be blessed. We are not to be surprised at painful trials taking place even while we are doing the right thing. The criterion of truly living the Christian life is not a life "free from trials, tribulations, sufferings, and afflictions."

> Always be prepared to give an answer to everyone who asks you to give the reason for the hope that you have. But do this with gentleness and respect, keeping a clear conscience, so that those who speak maliciously against your good behavior in Christ may be ashamed of their slander. (vv. 15, 16)

So there is the possibility that even those who slander us or give a false witness against us may be changed by our actions as well as our words.

Jesus bore false accusations and false witness for us. One of the worst sufferings I can imagine that Jesus had was to be falsely accused of not being the Son of God. He died because of a false testimony, as He had done no wrong thing; yet His accusers were able to get a judgment against Him. In dying for us, He took the false accusation for us and bore the penalty which belonged to us, not to Him. What an amazing exchange! He was actually dying so that some of those who were falsely accusing Him could have everlasting life because of His death. Think of Paul at that time! Where was he among the crowd of Jewish leaders?

Satan would like to get any one of us to falsely accuse God. He tries to entice us by sending darts of affliction which are so painful we are tempted to stop trusting God, or to blame God for being unfair to us. We know this from the book of Job and from Revelation. Satan had told God Job would curse Him to His face if he, Satan, could strike him with afflictions. Remember we are told in Job 1:22, "In all this, Job did not sin by charging God with wrong-doing."

In all what? Job's children had all just been killed by a mighty wind blowing the roof of their house down on them, and before that his cattle had all been stolen. One calamity after another had taken place. We are shown that Satan was trying to get Job to "charge God," to "curse God." Or, we could put it in the words of the ninth commandment, for Satan was really trying to "frame Job," to frame him into giving a false testimony against God to anyone who cared to listen!

We know from the book of Revelation that Satan has been doing the same kind of thing through the ages, and is still doing it, and will be doing it until that historic date in the future when he will be hurled down out of heaven, having had his last access to the throne of God. Satan is trying continually to make you and me speak out in a false accusation, a false testimony against God. He is trying to make us say before the angels and before demons, and before any human beings who may be listening to us, that God has been doing wrong things. He wants to make us sin by doing what he tried to make Job do—"charging God with wrongdoing." Whatever the affliction we have been hit with, however deeply we have been burdened with sorrows and troubles, the greatest loyalty we can demonstrate to God, and the greatest "witness" we can be on that particular witness stand, is to keep on being a true witness to who He is and to His perfect holiness and love and compassion.

We can take the words of Psalm 34:1-3 at such times and declare:

> I will extol the Lord at all times;
> his praise will always be on my lips.
> My soul will boast in the Lord;
> let the afflicted hear and rejoice.
> Glorify the Lord with me;
> let us exalt his name together.

10: THE TENTH COMMANDMENT

It can be said that the first commandment gives us a base for all the others. If we really had "no other gods before the One true God," if we completely loved Him and put Him before all else, we could be understanding and open-eyed concerning the meaning of all the other commandments. The first commandment gives a purpose, a reasonableness, to all the others. His existence as the Creator in whose image we are made makes it reasonable that He is the One who can give us the explanation about how to live in the light of who we are, in relationship to Him and to each other.

Just so, it can be said that the last commandment gives us an understanding of how we break all the others. The last commandment is the source of all sin, or one might say it is the preparation for all sin. In our illustration of the pickup sticks, this is the one stick that touches all the others. If one tried to pull it out the whole pile would shift.

The tenth commandment is the inside of the cup. The tenth commandment exists right where no other human being can see that it is being broken. But God is able to see. When the tenth commandment is being broken, other people may at that very moment be saying, "What a good person that is," "How fine a child that is," "What a good Christian she is." This is where it takes place—hidden from all eyes but God's.

Who are we? Each of us is one person, one human being, who exists in a place where no one but God, and our own self, knows what is going on. Each of us lives inside, in a very real way. Each of us is capable of being two people, doing one thing which people are observing, even saying one thing which people are hearing, and thinking and feeling a totally opposite thing, being schizophrenic with no one but ourselves and God being aware of it. Each of us has a struggle over some form of hypocrisy, and we are troubled in varying degrees about this situation. That is why so many are lying on couches in psychiatrists' offices.

The Apostle Paul verbalizes his own struggle in Romans 7 and helps us to see that it is the struggle of each one of us. The Old Testament points out the source of man's difficulty in living in this double manner, and gives us examples.

Just where is the location of our hidden life? Of what does the inside of the cup consist? It is very clear, without quibbling over terms, that both the "mind" and the "heart" are used in the Bible to indicate the thoughts, ideas, desires, motives, purposes, intentions, attitudes that exist as inward "seeds" which will, if allowed to remain planted within us, both grow into actions affecting other people and make known what had been hidden before. Our thought-world is the place where all sin begins, and is what God is reading as an open book, "seeing" as our ideas take shape within us, and "hearing" as if we had spoken it all audibly. God is the One who really knows who I am and who you are. He knows the *whole* person, both hidden and visible.

Come to the time when Samuel was picking one person to anoint as King, out of many brothers in the family God had indicated. There were many outward things to be seen by Samuel, or any others looking on, qualifications which looked great in the picking of such an important leader. Samuel was terrifically impressed with Eliab, and even thought to himself, "Surely this is the Lord's anointed." But God's reply to what Samuel was thinking is clearly given in 1 Samuel 16:7—

> But the Lord said to Samuel, "Do not consider his appearance or his height, for I have rejected him. The Lord does not look at the things man looks at. Man looks at the outward appearance, but God looks at the heart."

In 1 Kings 8:38, 39 we have in Solomon's prayer of dedication of the temple a glimpse of his understanding of the inner person, the hidden person whose thoughts the Lord alone sees.

". . . and when a prayer or plea is made by any of your people Israel—each one aware of the afflictions of his own heart, and spreading out his hands toward this temple—then hear from heaven, your dwelling place. Forgive and act; deal with each man according to all he does, since you know his heart (for you alone know the hearts of all men) . . ."

Jesus quoted from Isaiah to the Pharisees when He was telling them that they were hypocrites, that they were not inwardly what they appeared to be outwardly, nor what their lips said.

"Thus you nullify the word of God for the sake of your tradition. You hypocrites! Isaiah was right when he prophesied about you:

'These people honor me with their lips,
    but their hearts are far from me.
They worship me in vain;
    their teachings are but rules taught by men.' "
(Matthew 15:6-9)

It is the inside of the cup that Jesus was seeing as He stood saying these very words. He was actually seeing into the thoughts of their minds, into the intentions or motives of their words. Jesus knew the real intent of their questions and could read all the dishonesty that made what they said double talk.

If the first commandment had been a part of people's basic understanding of life, the last commandment would not have had to be the summing up of all sin. Romans 1:28 brings this into focus like a great searchlight brings out details in a dark garden. "Furthermore, since they did not think it worthwhile to retain the knowledge of God, he gave them over to a depraved mind, to do what ought not to be done."

If we push aside the knowledge of God and live without the Creator as a part of our understanding of the universe, of history, of our own existence, our mind (thoughts, heart, ideas, desires, motives, intents) becomes rapidly depraved. And depraved actions follow depraved minds. We see this in individuals, groups of people, villages, towns, cities, countries.

The tenth commandment really points out the source of all sin, and the breaking of the tenth commandment is primary to the breaking of the others. Jesus singles out this fact and makes it vivid when He says in Matthew 5:28—"But I tell you that anyone who looks at a woman lustfully has already committed adultery with her in his heart."

What is the tenth commandment?

"You shall not covet your neighbor's house. You shall not covet your neighbor's wife, or his manservant or maidservant, his ox or donkey, or any thing that belongs to your neighbor." (Exodus 20:17)

Deuteronomy 5:21 puts it this way:

"You shall not covet your neighbor's wife. You shall not set your desire on your neighbor's house or land, his manservant or maidservant, his ox or donkey, or anything that belongs to your neighbor."

Somewhere within our minds and hearts we have a continual struggle, and right there within our minds and hearts the victory may be won. There are temptations which do not become sin. Temptation can be turned from, not indulged in, even in our minds, where no one can be aware of what has gone on, except God Himself. There is a difference between temptation to covetousness and the sin of covetousness. There is a difference between admiring something and greedily wanting to take it away from the other person. There is a difference between simply admiring a neighbor's house, or bathroom, and designing the same kind of house, or bathroom, on paper, then earning the money or setting aside some from a legitimate source, in order to build something similar, and plotting to take something that belongs to someone else, feverishly bending all one's preparations to achieve that goal!

In Micah 2:1, 2 we have a description of those who covet and carry out their coveting in action.

> Woe to those who plan iniquity,
>   to those who plot evil on their beds!
> At morning's light they carry it out
>   because it is in their power to do it.
> They covet fields and seize them,
>   and houses, and take them.
> They defraud a man of his home,
>   a fellowman of his inheritance.

This is a graphic description of what happens when greedy lust for things comes into the mind and becomes predominant in the desires of the heart, turning what has been pictured in the thoughts into a passion to possess them at any cost.

The sin of coveting is so clearly basic. It is the easiest sin for us to recognize in ourselves if we are at all honest. Paul said very openly in Romans 7:7, 8, "I would not have known what sin was except through the law. For I would not have known what it was to covet if the law had not said, 'Do not covet.' But sin, seizing the opportunity afforded by the commandment, produced in me every kind of covetous desire." This is part of the whole background that makes Paul—and us—say time after time, "When I want to do good, evil is right there with me." We need to be aware of the sin of coveting, of all that can take place in our minds if we do not realize what it is we are in need of confessing, fighting against, and asking forgiveness for. And we must also realize what a hopeless state we would be in without the blood of Christ. If we don't understand something of the sinfulness of sin, we can't really appreciate the wonder of being forgiven.

Jesus in talking to some of the Pharisees and some of the teachers of the law who had come from Jerusalem to gather around Him began to tell them the ridiculous lack of understanding they had about sin. He told them how really upside down their standards and sense of values were. They were judging other people and being satisfied with themselves on the basis of keeping all sorts of little laws concerning what they would eat, how they would wash, and so on. Throwing ice water into their faces with words that should have shocked them into awareness, Jesus said,

> "Listen to me, everyone, and understand this. Nothing outside a man can make him 'unclean' by going into him. Rather, it is what comes out of a man that makes him 'unclean.' "
>
> After he had left the crowd and entered the house, his disciples asked him about this parable. "Are you so dull?" he asked. "Don't you see that nothing that enters a man from the outside can make him 'unclean'? For it doesn't go into his heart but into his stomach, and then out of his body." (In saying this, Jesus declared all foods "clean.")
>
> He went on: "What comes out of a man is what makes him 'unclean.' For from within, out of men's hearts, come evil thoughts, sexual immorality, theft, murder, adultery, greed, malice, deceit, lewdness, envy, slander, arrogance, and folly. All these evils come from inside and make a man 'unclean.' " (Mark 7:14-23)

Is it any wonder we are told that if we break one commandment, we are guilty of all? The commandments are tied together, woven into one pile of sticks leaning on each other; and all of them begin inside in the thought-world, in the mind and heart. Covetousness is the beginning, and it takes many, many forms.

In Colossians 3:5, in a paragraph urging us to "put on the new self, which is being renewed in knowledge in the image of its Creator," we are told, "Put to death, therefore, whatever belongs to your earthly nature: sexual immorality, impurity, lust, evil desires and greed (or covetousness), which is idolatry."

So here we are back in the second commandment! We have a definition now which helps us to see that when we begin to covet a three-thousand-acre ranch, or gorgeous race horses, or a jet plane, or an attractive young woman or man, or someone else's life-style, or a perfect house—whether a two-hundred-year-old one filled with historic antiques or an amazing modern one with a push-button possibility of living in ease—we are at the same time putting something else in God's place, we are bowing before an idol. The ranch, the horses, the plane, the woman or man, the life-style, the house, or whatever it is has slipped into the place of God. We are in the midst of idol worship without recognizing it or admitting to it. This is a subtle temptation indeed and one which reminds us again of Satan's wheedling temptations to Jesus, "Just bow for a minute, and all this will be yours." Satan tries to put anything he can in the place of our constant faithfulness to putting the Lord first. He attempts to put a great diversity of things there—especially things we won't recognize!

When the crowd was around Jesus, so thick that people were trampling on one another, someone in the crowd said to him, "Teacher, tell my brother to divide the inheritance with me" (Luke 12:13). Jesus' reply was, "Watch out! Be on your guard against all kinds of greed; a man's life does not consist in the abundance of his possessions" (verse 15).

It was after that that Jesus told the story of the man who had pulled down his barns to build more because he was storing up so many possessions in order to say to himself, "Take life easy; eat, drink and be merry."

"But God said to him, 'You fool! This very night your life will be demanded from you. Then who will get what you have prepared for yourself?' This is how it will be with anyone who stores up things for himself but is not rich toward God." (Luke 12:20, 21)

There are many warnings that the things which start within our own minds, our ideas, our ambitions, our desires, our motives are the very things that have the power to destroy us by twisting us into doing the things that do not fit in with what God made us to do and are therefore not fulfilling in the end at all.

We need to pray earnestly with the Psalmist, right now, before we read further:

> Direct me in the path of your commands,
> for there I find delight.
> Turn my heart toward your statutes
> and not toward selfish gain.
> Turn my eyes away from worthless things;
> renew my life according to your word.
> (Psalm 119:35-37)

Our constant prayer, interlaced through all the rest as we search and research God's Word, should be to check up on ourselves, to judge ourselves so we won't have to be judged.

In Ephesians 5 Paul is urging the Ephesians to live consistently with what they believe as Christians. The word "covetous" in the *King James Version* has been translated "greedy" in the *New International Version*, but read and see that clearly both are forms of idolatry.

For of this you can be sure: No immoral, impure or greedy person (covetous man)—such a man is an idolater—has any inheritance in the kingdom of Christ and of God. Let no one deceive you with empty words, for because of such things God's wrath comes on those who are disobedient. Therefore do not be partners with them. For you were once darkness, but now light in the Lord. Live as children of light (for the fruit of the light consists in all goodness, righteousness and truth) and find out what pleases the Lord.

We are told later in this same chapter to be careful how we live, because the days are evil. If this was true in the time Paul wrote to the Ephesians, it is just as true now. Rather than having gone "out of date," this is very much in keeping with what we need as we live in the mess of the twentieth century. Have you read today's paper? Have you read this week's news magazine? Have you read reports of what is going on in the way of sin and violence among nations and among unbelievers, but also among those who are in the church and even among leaders of the Christian organizations? What kind of a day are we living in when light and darkness so often are mixed in a foggy grey souplike atmosphere—something like the worst smog you have ever driven through!

We who are Christians, we who are the only representatives on earth of the living God, the Creator of heaven and earth, the One who made people in His image, are meant to be salt and light. We are meant to preserve at least something of righteousness, and we are meant to be lights that show up in the smog! Where are we? What kinds of covetousness are keeping us from having the courage to call our particular idols idols? What kind of rationalizing is causing us to neglect to call sin sin in our own thought-world or in the actions that are going on all around us? How are our lives conforming to all that is going on around us, so that we melt into the smog without any difference in color making us stand out? How could anyone tell us apart from all the other idol worshipers?

We may not be tempted to bow down to any kind of religious idol or to take part in false worship of any sort, and we may be fully aware of the dangers of the occult or the cults that spring up overnight these days. But we *are* in need of inspecting our lives to check up on what might have come in which is not what God would have it be.

Motives are so tricky. We can go to the mission field with the purest of motives, certain that God has led us there, desirous of bringing glory to Him as well as bringing His truth to whatever people He puts us in touch with. And then a shift can come. Pride comes in, and within the mind and heart a raging desire to be first can enter in, even as it did with the disciples. There can be the drive to be the best in language, the most spiritual in taking more days of fasting and prayer than anyone else, or in getting up earlier to pray. Not that any of these things are wrong; it is the *motive* that can suddenly shift, and the desire of being thought of as a success by the people back in the home church can replace the desire of pleasing the Lord or bringing Him joy.

We can be pastor or leader in a church, elder, or Sunday school teacher and have a covetous desire to be outstanding—not for the right motives, but for selfish motives and for some twisted lust for honor and recognition. The motives can slip out of place without our being aware of it, and we can feel secure in our own pious life, thinking we are really doing everything with a kind of self-sacrificial willingness, when after all we have been deceiving ourselves as well as others. God, who can see the shift and who sees the inside of the cup, may be the only one aware of the unclean situation which exists there.

However, there are more blatant kinds of covetousness among those who have been, and are, leaders of God's people. Jeremiah reports what the Lord says not only for that time of history but for ours too:

> This is what the Lord Almighty says: . . .
> "From the least to the greatest,
>   all are greedy for gain;
> prophets and priests alike,
>   all practice deceit.
> They dress the wound of my people
>   as though it were not serious.
> 'Peace, peace,' they say,
>   when there is no peace."
>   (Jeremiah 6:9, 13, 14)

What a shocking description! It sends goosebumps over our flesh. "They dress the wound of my people as though it were not serious." How awful it is to God to have people sitting on benches, in chairs, on pews, waiting to hear what He has to say to them, only to be given teaching that is trivial, that does not at all hit the reality of the need of hungry people who are wounded by the fallenness of the world, torn apart by sin, and looking for answers to their serious need.

The soothing voices and religious music playing softly in the background do nothing to meet the serious needs. All that comes into the ears is a crooning of peace, peace, when God says there is no peace, but a battle that is continuing until Jesus comes back. Warriors are to be called into the battle, prepared to fight. The enemy, Satan, is to meet opposition, not people lulled to sleep with the soporific drugs of religiosity rocking them into a place where they don't want their peace disturbed. It becomes peace at any cost, a covetous lust for being undisturbed, left alone to enjoy life. It is just as covetous a lust as the lust for the neighbor's wife or someone else's life or the land that belongs to another. This is not our time of rest and sleep. We are told not to sleep, but to be alert in the warfare in which we are engaged.

Come back to Jeremiah's time for a moment. Here are a people being spoken to who have forsaken God and have served other gods. Remember that covetousness is a form of idolatry and that Satan would like us to covet peace now. He does not want us to engage in the battle against him, but to sleep until our lives are over and we can no longer do anything that would affect him.

God speaks about Shallum, son of Josiah, who succeeded his father as king of Judah, but who was far, far from putting the Lord first and was full of covetousness in a variety of forms.

> "Woe to him who builds his palace by unrighteousness,
>   his upper rooms by injustice,
> making his countrymen work for nothing,
>   not paying them for their labor.
> He says, 'I will build myself a great palace
>   with spacious upper rooms.'
> So he makes large windows in it,
>   panels it with cedar
>   and decorates it in red.
> Does it make you a king
>   to have more and more cedar?
> Did not your father have food and drink?
>   He did what was right and just,
>   so all went well with him.
> He defended the cause of the poor and needy,
>   and so all went well.
> Is that not what it means to know me?"
>   declares the Lord.
> "But your eyes and your heart
>   are set only on dishonest gain,
> on shedding innocent blood
>   and on oppression and extortion."
>   (Jeremiah 22:13-17)

Is this not a time to speak out strongly, as strongly as in the day of Jeremiah? It is a time to declare what is going on which is an abomination in the eyes of God—not a time to seek for a sleepy, soothing kind of message. Today, innocent blood is being shed for economic reasons, and a great variety of oppression is taking place. Today is the time when we are to listen to Romans 13:11, 12.

> And do this [referring to the statement that love is the fulfillment of the law], understanding the present time. The hour has come for you to wake up from your slumber, because our salvation is nearer now than when we first believed. The night is nearly over, the day is almost here. So let us put aside the deeds of darkness and put on the armor of light.

The loud and clear message to us is—Wake up! Wake up because Jesus' coming is closer than it was the day we believed. Therefore, we are not to go to sleep thinking our perfection is so close we don't need to do a single thing but sing and wait for that great day. Quite the opposite!

We are to wake up and put on our armor. Armor is for a battle! We ought to be extremely eager to find out what the armor consists of and what we are supposed to be doing. Surely if people in Jeremiah's time were punished for not defending the cause of the poor and needy, and for not defending the innocent whose blood should not be shed, should we who have been changed into children of light through accepting Christ as Savior be doing *less*? That doesn't make sense.

We should be the ones defending the causes of the poor and needy. We should be the ones speaking out against shedding innocent blood. We should be the ones decrying oppression and extortion, whether it is being carried on by one person, a small group, or an authoritarian government. We should be ready to do something about setting free those who are in chains and are calling for help in such countries.

Coveting peace and affluence, coveting constant happiness at the cost of breaking up a home to find a "better" husband or wife, with children paying the price, coveting sexual fulfillment with no thought of God's commandments, coveting power whether the power of a great political leader or the power of being the president of a church society of ten people, coveting spiritual experiences for the excitement or the feeling or the possibility of reporting something to a group, coveting leadership of a group large or small with authority to tell others what to do—whatever the coveting consists of, it is sin, and the results when the coveting becomes action are a multiplication of that sin.

Ezekiel describes great varieties of covetousness as he tells what God told him to tell the people in Ezekiel 33:31.

> "My people come to you, as they usually do, and sit before you to listen to your words, but they do not put them into practice. With their mouths they express devotion, but their hearts are greedy for unjust gain."

No one has ever been able to fool God. There is no way to hide one's thoughts and greedy desires, one's motives or contrary feelings of rebellion which are going on during the time "mouths . . . express devotion." The lid is off! He knows what is going on in the hearts.

Where are we? Where are you? Where am I?

First we are to take seriously God's law. It is important to turn a listening ear to Him and to ask His help as we hear and consider where we fall short. Proverbs 28:9 tells us,

> "If anyone turns a deaf ear to the law,
> even his prayers are detestable."

But when we recognize how prone we are to fall short of keeping the law, we need to be reassured of exactly what Christ did for us. Paul relates something of his own struggles and points out the solution.

> So I find this law at work: When I want to do good, evil is right there with me. . . . What a wretched man I am! Who will rescue me from this body of death? Thanks be to God—through Jesus Christ our Lord! So then, I myself in my mind am a slave to God's law, but in the sinful nature a slave to the law of sin! . . . Therefore, there is no condemnation for those who are in Christ Jesus, because through Christ Jesus the law of the Spirit of life set me free from the law of sin and death. For what the law was powerless to do in that it was weakened by the sinful nature, God did by sending his own Son in the likeness of sinful man to be a sin offering. And so he condemned sin in sinful man, in order that the righteous requirements of the law might be fully met in us, who do not live according to the sinful nature but according to the Spirit. (Romans 7:21, 24, 25; 8:1-4)

Do any of us have any real concept of what the death of Christ cost God the Father, Christ Himself, and the Holy Spirit? What a terrible price was paid so that we could be told we would not be condemned for all we have done!

And it is true.

Now we can go back once again to Romans 13, and read what just preceded the admonition to put on the armor of light.

> Let no debt remain outstanding, except the continuing debt to love one another, for he who loves his fellow man has fulfilled the law. The commandments, "Do not commit adultery," "Do not murder," "Do not steal," "Do not covet," and whatever other commandment there may be, are summed up in this one rule, "Love your neighbor as yourself." Love does no harm to its neighbor. Therefore love is the fulfillment of the law. (Romans 13:8-10)

If we loved God with all our hearts and minds and souls, we would love our neighbors as ourselves. And if we loved our neighbors in this complete way, we would not do anything to harm them. You see, it is all tied up together. And it makes sense. The truth of what exists and the truth about who we are and what will fulfill us is tied in with our everyday, moment-by-moment living.

In Ephesians 4 Paul urges believers, including us, to be consistent with who we are now that we are restored to being in relationship with God.

> . . . I urge you to live a life worthy of the calling you have received. Be completely humble, gentle; be patient, bearing with one another in love. . . . Then we will no longer be infants, tossed back and forth by the waves and blown here and there by every wind of teaching and by the cunning and craftiness of men in their deceitful scheming. Instead, speaking the truth in love, we will in all things grow up into him who is the Head, that is, Christ. From him the whole body, joined and held together by every supporting ligament, grows and builds itself up in love, as each part does its work. (vv. 1, 2, 14-16)

That is the positive portion. Now we come to the negative part— what we are not to do!

> So I tell you this, and insist on it in the Lord, that you must no longer live as the Gentiles do, in the futility of their thinking. They are darkened in their understanding and separated from the life of God because of the ignorance that is in them due to the hardening of their

hearts. Having lost all sensitivity, they have given themselves over to sensuality so as to indulge in every kind of impurity, with a continual lust for more.

This is a brilliant warning, explicit as to what Christians are to not be like. Within the Christian family, church, mission, assembly, group there is not meant to be covetousness, which is described here as a sensuality which indulges every kind of impurity with a continual lust for more. Yet tragically this sounds like a description of what is going on not just outside the people of God, but among those who name the name of Christ.

It is to this same group of Christians in Ephesus that the end of the letter spells out the only way to "put on the armor" which will make a difference in day-by-day life. We are not only battling our inward self who at times would try to make us be a dirty cup inside while we are outwardly smiling and saying the right words; we also have an enemy who is attacking us. We need the armor to fight him. See Ephesians 6:10-20.

Finally, be strong in the Lord and in his mighty power.
    [Note that we are offered His strength in our weakness many times; this is urging us to act on promises!]
Put on the full armor of God so that you can take your stand against the devil's schemes.
    [The devil has schemes. This is God's Word telling us so. We need armor to protect us against the schemes.]
  For our struggle is not against flesh and blood, but against the rulers, against the authorities, against the powers of this dark world and against the spiritual forces of evil in the heavenly realms.
    [What a struggle! It is a present tense. We are in this struggle. It is important, and it is continual. We need help. Who do we think we are if we think we can take on all the forces of evil, the devil himself and his demons aligned against us, in our own strength and with our own cleverness?]
  Therefore put on the full armor of God, so that when the day of evil comes, you may be able to stand your ground, and after you have done everything, to stand.
    [The "day of evil" will not be announced in time to get ready for it. We are meant to be prepared all the time for the moment it sneaks up on us, so we can stand!]
Stand firm then, with the belt of truth buckled around your waist, with the breastplate of righteousness in place, and with your feet fitted with the readiness that comes from the gospel of peace.

[Truth matters! It is important to have truth buckled firmly in place. It is not an *experience* which is sufficient, but a firm circle of *truth* that you can count on to stay in place. Then comes the breastplate of righteousness—yes, the righteousness of Christ covers us, but we know what that righteousness consists of when we understand the Ten Commandments better. Then our feet are fitted with the readiness that comes from the good news that our sins are forgiven in Christ, a peaceful assurance indeed with which to run!]

In addition to all this, take up the shield of faith, with which you can extinguish all the flaming arrows of the evil one.

[The object of our faith is the One on whom we can count. He never changes, and we can be certain that nothing is impossible to Him. He to whom nothing is impossible can make sure that when those flaming arrows are flying thick and fast at us, they are extinguished as we call upon Him in faith. We have a mean antagonist, but a powerful ally.]

Take the helmet of salvation and the sword of the Spirit, which is the word of God.

[How do we take the helmet of salvation? By being certain that we have really accepted what Christ has done for us as He died on the cross at such great cost and have not tried to add anything to that for our salvation, but have thanked Him for doing it all for us. And the sword of the Spirit? Daily we need to take the Word of God, reading, meditating, and doing as we are instructed. We need to use it not only in defense, but also in offensive attack against our enemies' lies.]

And pray in the Spirit on all occasions with all kinds of prayers and requests.

[The call to prayer is a part of the putting on of the armor. We are not protected in the battle without prayer. It is a part of the defense, but also of the offense. We have access to the Top General at any moment in asking for help, in asking for wisdom in making choices, in bringing our admiration and thanks for all that has been and is being done for us—and we can make requests! How important it is on the battlefield to be in constant communication with the General, with Headquarters!]

With this in mind, be alert and always keep on praying for all the saints.

[We are to keep in mind that praying in the power of the indwelling Holy Spirit is not just a privilege we have for ourselves so that we can keep our heads above water when the waves get high— for this is a sea battle too—but in the midst of the storm or during a time of calmer waters we can and must intercede for others. We are told it is not an optional affair. In this battle we are together, and what affects one of us affects all of us. So we are not to go to sleep after we have prayed for ourselves. We are to be alert and pray for all the saints. In this battle when so many are being shot down and seem to be in the mud, we are to be praying for them to help them get up. There is a definite responsibility connected with the full armor and with the battle against Satan. It is not a time to be asleep. The disciples slept when Jesus was going through *His* titanic struggle in the Garden of Gethsemane. We are called upon to stay awake in this battle, not to just live for peace and pleasure, but to be alert to each other's needs, as well as our own, in the face of an enemy.]

Pray also for me, that whenever I open my mouth, words may be given me so that I will fearlessly make known the mystery of the gospel, for which I am an ambassador in chains. Pray that I may declare it fearlessly, as I should.

[Dear, dear Paul. No pride in his ability to use the right words. No shame in asking for prayer not to be fearful. Paul asks for prayer that God would give him the right words. We are reminded of the promise which Paul would well remember, when Jeremiah was promised the words with which to speak. Not only was Paul in chains, but he had been stoned and suffered bruises and scars from the stoning. He also had stripes from three terrible beatings. With all he had reason to fear as a result of not stopping, Paul asks for special prayer that he would keep on declaring the truth fearlessly. This is what the battle is all about and why the armor is needed. Anyone who shuts up and lets no one know what he or she believes is not a threat to the enemy. We are meant to put our armor on and to plunge in!]

We need to know the Ten Commandments—because our enemy Satan, the devil, knows them well. Satan knows what the laws are that he wants us to break. Satan is trying to destroy any change that might take place in the life of a Christian, so he shoots his flaming arrows at vulnerable spots. He begins at the beginning. Clever Enemy! He is well aware that covetousness is the beginning of our breaking other commandments, as well as the tenth.

Knowing that we are going to be attacked, knowing that we need armor to protect ourselves, being well warned that Satan walks to and fro seeking whom he may devour, we are really stupid if we do not study well the Ten Commandments and prepare ourselves for the areas of attack, recognizing them when they come.

Does it sound easier to say all the commandments are summed up in loving God with heart and mind and soul, and loving our neighbor as ourselves? Does it sound easier to say that love is the fulfillment of the law? No. To the extent that we are not keeping the Ten Commandments we are not loving!

Consider 1 Corinthians 13:4-8.

> Love is patient, love is kind. It does not envy, it does not boast, it is not proud. It is not rude, it is not self-seeking, it is not easily angered, it keeps no record of wrongs. Love does not delight in evil but rejoices with the truth. It always protects, always trusts, always hopes, always perseveres. Love never fails.

God gave the Ten Commandments to the people He had made in His image so they could understand who they are, how to live with each other, and how to live in communication with Himself. They have been broken for centuries, but they remain what they have always been, a guide for living in the light of what really is, what truth is, what the cosmos is, who we are, and who God the Creator is.